M000298469

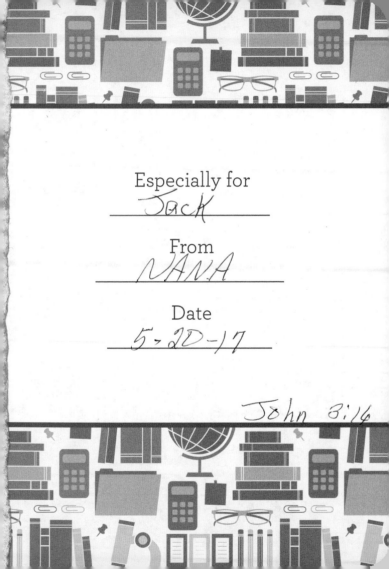

Especially for

Jack

From

NANA

Date

_5-20-17_

John 8:16

3-MINUTE DEVOTIONS FOR GRADS

Inspiring Devotions and Prayers

BARBOUR BOOKS
An Imprint of Barbour Publishing, Inc.

INTRODUCTION

Graduation marks a unique milestone. Beyond the investment of time and energy already expended, this event signifies an accomplishment of amazing proportions. Starting something is easy, but finishing—and finishing well—shows that you are a person of remarkable perseverance. The most exciting thing about graduation day is that it doesn't just mark an ending but opens the door wide to a new beginning.

As you take the next steps on a lifelong journey, so many options are open to you. This is the time for moving ahead in positive directions. Developing a deeper relationship with God and finding more time for Bible study and prayer are both habits worth strengthening.

Congratulations, Graduate! You are amazing—and God has many wonderful things in store for you!

You make known to me the path of life;
you will fill me with joy in your presence,
with eternal pleasures at your right hand.

PSALM 16:11 NIV

SPINNING OUR WHEELS

*Let us move beyond the elementary teachings
about Christ and be taken forward to maturity.*
HEBREWS 6:1 NIV

Procrastination is one of the most difficult forces
to overcome. We know we have to get started on
something but then find ourselves moving in slow
motion. Slowing down—stopping—doing nothing.
Remember when this happened in school?

Maybe there is a big project coming up. The
thought of starting a huge task can sometimes be
enough to put us in frozen mode. Though we know
we need to dig in, instead we wait, and wait some
more. Or we find ways to distract ourselves from
what definitely needs to be done. We organize our
pen drawer, fold our underwear, or clean the tile
grout. Anything and everything becomes more
appealing than doing what we must. Even heroes
suffer from this kind of temporary sluggishness.
Few soldiers long to lunge back into battle, but they
know that they must. They realize that putting off the
inevitable will not improve the situation but, in fact,
make matters worse.

By comparison, our reasons for slipping into slow gear seem paltry. Do we just feel tired? Are we annoyed about not getting the credit for a project that we feel we deserve? Any number of good and valid explanations can pull at us; they stop us from trying our hardest until we get the attention that should be ours.

Is that what God would have us do? That is pretty doubtful. Let's take every opportunity to move ahead, to advance, especially when our work is for the Kingdom. Rather than letting our wheels spin or standing still, we should be straining to reach our good goals. We should prayerfully do all that is in our power to show that our attitude, our work, and our drive is exceptional because we draw our motivation from a heavenly source.

Lord, sometimes I feel so tired. I don't want to keep trying, but I know I must. Give me the energy and strength I need to accomplish the small but mighty things You have for me to do. Amen.

HANDLING LIFE 101

*A person might have to suffer even
when it is unfair, but if he thinks of God
and can stand the pain, God is pleased.*
1 PETER 2:19 NCV

Every day provides chances to grow emotionally,
physically, and spiritually. Whether or not we take
advantage of such opportunities is another question
entirely. We may wake up ready to take on the world—
or at least promptly get out of bed—and then find that
we've overslept, *really* overslept. Suddenly the perfect
day is ruined. In the rush to dress, our clothes don't
match and bed head is the best we can manage. How
do we handle this negative stuff? Pretend? Act tough
and pretend that nothing's wrong? But don't those
options just make things worse?

Stumbling along, we trip over an untied shoelace.
A bloody nose drips on an expensive new shirt. We're
ready to blow our top. Nothing is going right. At all!

We might wish it were otherwise, but bad days
do happen, sometimes frequently. Add in messed-up
communication with a loved one, a broken-down car,
or someone getting sick, and we have the perfect

recipe for over-the-top stress. Unless we discover how to keep trying even when things are falling apart, we're heading for more trouble.

Here's a survival plan. Take a deep breath, take a walk, and get a drink of water. Go somewhere. Anywhere. Get out of that exhausting space. The change of scenery alone will help bring us focus. It will also provide momentum toward change. Sometimes we seem to prefer our deep rut to the unknown we fear. We need to get over that kind of thinking. The best course is to confidently believe that things will change, maybe even get a whole lot better. But we can't give up when the going gets tough. No matter what, with the right attitude, things will improve.

God, I don't know if I can deal with another day like I just had. It was a tough one. Please give me the strength I need to keep trying even when things keep going wrong. I'm glad You're here for me. Amen.

EXCELLENCE VS. PERFECTION

We all stumble in many ways.
Anyone who is never at fault in what they say
is perfect, able to keep their whole body in check.
JAMES 3:2 NIV

Some people spend their lives trying to appear perfect. From personal hygiene, hair, clothes, shoes, belts, and other accessories to having the perfect car, the "perfect" people can't stand to have a thing out of place. That's because they gain their identity and their value by having people compliment them on the externals. Such creeping perfection infects how they view everything from where they live, who they'll talk to, and what jobs they will accept, to what books, music, and movies they will enjoy.

They will partake only in what the "powers that be" have proclaimed to be good, right, and cool. Very often they spend countless hours chasing down the smallest, most insignificant details so that they can present themselves as top notch, the ultimate, and just plain perfect, though few actually notice their hard efforts. No one else cares as much as the person obsessing.

Now excellence is a whole different matter. This is the pursuit of something much more important. It is the desire to do what's necessary with efficiency and quality. But if there's a wrinkle in the pants, that person won't refuse to go outside. They won't be crushed by what others think. No. They're going to enjoy doing their best because it makes them feel good. An excellent job is a noble goal, but striving for perfection can push us over the edge.

Let's take stock of where we land on the scale. Since graduation, have we made an effort toward excellence and growth with each attempt? Or have we set our sights on absolute perfection and brought on personal failure because we can't reach our outrageous goals? It's time to stop striving for the impossible. Just take long strides toward self-improvement rather than worrying about self-perfection.

Lord, I want to do my very best,
but I want to do it for the right reason.
Help me to stop acting like I must be perfect to
be accepted, and help me to know that serving
You wholeheartedly is all that matters. Amen.

WORDS OF TRUTH

These are the things which you should do:
speak the truth to one another; judge with truth
and judgment for peace in your gates.
ZECHARIAH 8:16 NASB

What makes it so tough to believe people
sometimes? Maybe because we've trusted too often
and been burned more than once. People promised
us this or that or told us that they'd follow through in
some particular way, but didn't. Maybe some former
classmates let us down. Either they were telling us
what we wanted to hear or were flat-out lying to our
faces. Another more charitable possibility is that they
weren't carefully matching their intentions with their
available time and resources. They didn't mean to lie
and they wanted to please us, but they didn't count
the cost of the vows they made.

Throughout life we have many chances to shade
the truth—that is, to tell things our way, with our spin.
We want to make ourselves look a bit better than
the facts warrant. We all do it, but that doesn't make
it right. The better option is to work to be a man or
woman of integrity, to be the person others can rely on.

Of course, honesty isn't always what people want. In fact, that's one real reason that so many people get wishy-washy in certain situations. They don't want to give bad news. They're afraid of hurting someone's feelings or being disliked. Truth is a tough burden to bear, but it's the only way that people will ever find out what matters in life—and what matters to us.

We should all strive to be that one person everyone believes. The person to be counted on to always tell the truth. It can be done if we're beyond being bought or manipulated. To do that, we must know right from wrong and choose the right, no questions asked.

Lord, it's hard to speak the truth sometimes. Really hard. People like to hear what makes them feel good. Please help me to be a force for what's right even if it's difficult. Amen.

GOING FOR THE GOLD

Seek first the kingdom of God and His righteousness,
and all these things shall be added to you.
MATTHEW 6:33 NKJV

We've all heard this advice before: get good grades,
find the top jobs, and make lots of money. These and
other mantras of success have filled our heads since
we were young. Glossy advertisements continually
show us a place, a lifestyle, a relationship, a gadget—
something we're missing. Without those vital things,
we're told, we won't obtain wholeness and happiness.
For example, we admire the athletes who reach for
the stars and grab gold. We then watch as they sell
toothpaste and deodorant. The message is clear:
use this toothpaste or smear on that deodorant so
we'll be loved and successful like these superstars.

We know in reality that there aren't enough gold
medals to go around. And if there were, if everyone
got a prize, it would cheapen the accomplishment
of those who have worked so hard to achieve
extraordinary success. We can strive to improve in
any arena, from sewing to swimming, and yet we
don't have to be the top pro to have fun, to make

friends, and to get some healthy exercise. Learning is what is important. Just as important are keeping an active mind, taking journeys, striving for more, and living without fear. It's definitely okay to make an attempt and fall short, just so long as we keep trying.

Whenever we see an opportunity to veer out of the comfort zone, let's take it. The world isn't looking for those who sit and watch TV on the couch. No one needs one more person with a hand outstretched, seeking something for nothing. Rather, we can be a part of a small group that puts service to others above selfish gain. We must be the person who isn't afraid of anything. When we're going for medals, let's grasp for the only gold that really matters.

O, Lord, please help me to keep my priorities in order. Help me to see what really matters and to do what's right in Your sight. Give me new opportunities to serve You and others and to sharpen my focus. Amen.

HOW YOU FRAME IT

Stand firm, and you will win life.
LUKE 21:19 NIV

———

Framing someone's artwork is an art in and of itself. A frame can enhance what's at its center: a photo of a big-eyed baby, a painted sunrise, or a paw print of a favorite pup. But if the frame doesn't fit, the whole effect is ruined. Instead of noticing the beauty of the art, we can only see how tacky the edging is!

Each of us has the chance to frame our words, our actions, our lives in ways that draw attention to us. Or we can choose to point to God. If we want people to be attracted to our faith, we should not distract them with our hard edges or cutting lines. Just like in school, we were attracted by honesty. When we are hoping to lead someone to trust in the Creator, we shouldn't cover up our good intentions with gaudy trimmings.

One reason for frames is to provide strength and support around something fragile and delicate. Around something that needs protection. Think of the artwork in this context as the softness of the soul. We want to highlight the light within, to create a frame that serves its purpose but that also complements who the artist is as a person; to show us both the beauty of the creation and the Creator.

Throughout life we should build and strengthen the beauty of the soul. As believers we are also building a frame that says something about who we are and what we stand for and whether or not we should be taken seriously. Our well-chosen border shows how much we care. Most of all, the way we frame our life points to who is at the center of it, and it highlights the beauty of our faith, our creativity, our strength, and our ability to love.

Lord, please let my whole being point the way to You. Show me how I can best show Your love living and thriving within me. Give me opportunities to draw others to Your beauty, Your majesty, and Your creation. Amen.

LADIES AND GENTLEMEN

Do not conform to the pattern of this world,
but be transformed by the renewing of your mind.
Then you will be able to test and approve
what God's will is—his good,
pleasing and perfect will.
ROMANS 12:2 NIV

The words "ladies and gentlemen" almost sound like something from another century or maybe an old black-and-white movie. It's a shame, but today we don't hear much talk encouraging men and women to act like gentlemen and ladies. What does that really mean anyway?

It means putting someone else first and doing the best we can to show kindness even when it would be much easier to ignore the needs of another. It means letting a frantic driver merge in front of us though technically we have the right to plow ahead. These are the surface things, the easy things. In actuality, these civilized and polite behaviors should already be second nature to a mature adult. At a deeper level, being a lady or gentleman is also about thoughtfulness. We want to strive to think before acting. Not content to do or say the first thing that pops into our heads, we first consider how our words and actions will impact others. Then we choose the right response, not because we have to or because others expect it but because of who we are and the fact that we respect others.

Ladies and gentlemen do small things that show respect. They look someone in the eye when they are speaking. They show respect to a teacher. They listen politely and carefully without interrupting. They are considerate and attuned to the feelings of others. Finally, spiritually grounded ladies and gentlemen know what they believe and stick to those principles even when others cave in to peer pressure. Let's strive to be honorable ladies or gentlemen, people who are just and caring. Since such people are so rare, our consistent kindness will shine as brightly as a flare in the darkness.

God, it is a challenge to do what's proper and appropriate in this world. It's much easier to muddle through the day, putting myself first, grabbing instead of giving. Please give me moment-by-moment opportunities to serve others with gentleness. Amen.

ROLE MODELS WANTED

You yourselves, as living stones,
are being built into a spiritual house
for a holy priesthood to offer spiritual sacrifices
acceptable to God through Jesus Christ.
1 PETER 2:5 HCSB

What role models do we most admire? It's a long list that includes singers, sports figures, movie stars, and good old superheroes. Take Superman. He's a classic role model who has been around for generations. But does that make him worth following?

We imagine ourselves in an exciting role, up front, onstage. We're intrigued by the work performers do and who they are—or seem to be. But that veneer is often quite thin. Many who have experienced meeting the headliner after a concert say they were hurt when that star could barely be bothered to shake their hand. Unfortunately, that's the way with many worldly "role models." They look good on the big screen but falter in real-world settings. That's not the kind of role models we need.

Instead, we should be alert for people who make a difference every day in consistent ways. Like the mom with small children who finds time to make a meal for a sick neighbor. Or like a dad who spends an hour throwing a ball with his kids even after a long, hard day. Or the friend who struggles to get good grades while working a part-time job and volunteering at the local homeless shelter. All of these real-life heroes are worth getting to know better.

They don't just talk about doing the right thing, they live out their beliefs and change lives in the process. Sure, it might be fun to fly through the air with a cape, but c'mon, how likely is that? Not very. Superheroes are pure fantasy, but role models are the real heroes. Let's find one worthy of our time and attention. Then one day, maybe we can become a hero to someone else. That's the way the story goes. Be a part of it.

Lord, help me seek out those who don't seek fame and attention. Show me these unsung heroes so that I can come alongside them and pray for them. And help me model my life on those who serve without seeking glory. Amen.

FIND REAL FRIENDS

The righteous choose their friends carefully,
but the way of the wicked leads them astray.
PROVERBS 12:26 NIV

Virtual friends are easy to come by. Especially in this world of instant messaging and social networking, we sometimes think that the number of friends we have matters more than the depth of those connections. But, if we think for a moment, do we really believe that someone can have hundreds (or millions!) of close friends? It's never worked that way before.

True friends come in different varieties. There are those people we enjoy doing things with like fellow volunteers, other students, or a team of mountain climbers. Or maybe a group of nervous new employees trapped in an elevator. Surface friendships flourish with people we're around, but real friends are much more than that. They're the ones who know our secrets and have stuck close despite mood swings, arguments, and moving across the country. We could call them anytime and they'd drop everything to help us.

How do we find the treasure of friendship? By

choosing carefully and avoiding connections just because of what we think they can do for us. We never pressure them to meet our needs or put our goals and happiness first. That's not what friendship is about. Real friends are the people we care about and who care back. One-sided friendships are an open invitation to be used.

If we give and give and give in the hope of being tossed a morsel of respect or praise, then there's something very wrong with the relationship. A real friend is someone we can trust, who asks the right questions. And who knows when to be quiet and listen. Such relationships are rare, but so are lifelong friends. Let's forget about trying to collect a bunch and, rather, invest in a few. That way we can spend decades tirelessly making those connections closer and more precious.

Lord, help me see that a true friend is a gift from You. Show me the relationships I should nurture and those I can let go. Most of all teach me how to be a true friend to others. Amen.

TRY NEW THINGS

Give instruction to a wise man,
and he will be still wiser; teach a just man,
and he will increase in learning.
PROVERBS 9:9 NKJV

Boredom or accomplishment? It's totally our choice. All we need to do is pick up a newspaper, go online to "activities" for our city, or tap into our church and we'll find an amazing number of groups and gatherings with which to get involved. Of course, we have to be open to new things and willing to follow up on invitations from others.

There's no limit to the number of new opportunities awaiting us. And each brings with it the chance to meet new people. Don't be afraid. It'll be all right even if we don't particularly enjoy those first awkward introductions. The more we practice, the easier such connections become. The best part is having the chance to discover other options for using our God-given talents. And the more things we try, the more surprising new skills and interests we may discover.

Maybe we've never balanced on a skateboard,

made a cookie from scratch, or volunteered at the animal shelter. That's not a problem! Nothing's stopping us from going for it now.

The bottom line is that boredom should be banned from our lives. We have so many ways to exercise, meet people, and help those in need if we're willing to take the first step. Go out on a limb and forget being worried or embarrassed. Burning away hours in mindless, repetitive pursuits (like video games or reruns on the tube) slashes our chances to grow and advance.

Even if we spend only a small, but regular, chunk of time every day learning a language, knitting a sweater, or jogging, improvement will come. This is one case where it's truly possible to get an "A" for effort. All we have to do is put aside our hesitations and fear of failure and watch our horizons expand.

Lord, thanks for opening so many doors for me,
and help me stop making excuses.
Please show me how to grow in my skills
and get past my fears of trying new things. Amen.

FEED YOUR SOUL

*Jesus replied: "Love the Lord your God
with all your heart and with all your
soul and with all your mind."*
MATTHEW 22:37 NIV

Our souls grow when nourished with faith and purpose. A well-fed soul is easily roused, not numb from lack of use. Still, at times we may try to ignore it if we've done something wrong. Lots of people do that. With practice, any of us can overlook things that should set our soul on edge.

When that occurs we lock our souls in a steel box. Imagine what happens when our souls are neglected like that. They shrivel and darken, and we find ourselves wandering further from the truth. Thankfully, when exposed to the light of mercy, hope, and joy, even a neglected soul can begin to blossom.

Some people find spiritual strength in the Bible or by attending church. Meeting with other believers can increase our confidence about our faith. Ultimately, making our own choices about the care of our souls is the same as making our own decisions about life and death, heaven and hell. In the busy rush of life we may leave our faith behind. Maybe even consider some crazy options. Forget those failures. Now's the time for us to move on in positive directions that bring sustenance to the starving soul.

Find faithful friends and family members who love God, and ask questions of them. If we have parents who are believers, they can be an incredible source of knowledge about how to stay spiritually grounded. They want to see us feed our souls as we mature. Those who pray for us will eagerly answer questions, talk of their own struggles to keep their faith strong, and help in any way they can. As we move past graduation, the constant careful tending of our souls should remain a top priority.

Lord, I sometimes forget how crucial it is to take good care of my soul. I know I need to do more. Please let me have opportunities to grow closer to You. Help me to head in a direction that draws me closer to You. Amen.

TAKE A TECH BREAK

*You shall rise up before the grayheaded
and honor the aged, and you shall
revere your God; I am the LORD.*
LEVITICUS 19:32 NASB

Today's technology wasn't even imagined less than a generation ago. And someday soon (like next year!) our state-of-the-art gadgets will seem ancient to others. But toying with all these devices limits our time in other pursuits. How many hours do we spend each day sharing, shopping, and surfing without ever getting out of our chairs? If we hushed these distractions, we might have a few moments of silence to think. We can even afford to turn off the television and nix the online movies once in a while.

For a change, we could crack open a book and read. Or sit down with a friend or family member, look them in the eye, and ask a question. Have a real first-person, in-the-flesh conversation—like people used to do in the olden days. We could even go for a walk around the block, visit an ailing neighbor, call an old school friend, fix a meal for a family welcoming a new baby, or pull the bike out of storage.

Technology can be marvelous if it shows us ways to connect more deeply and more meaningfully with the people in our lives. But if it merely serves to isolate us, then what's the point? We'd be far better off painting a picture than surfing the web. We could even use the extra time to learn to surf for real.

We shouldn't let ourselves become someone else's white noise. Let's get off the sofa and literally *do* something. Start a new trend! Forget the tech and go old-fashioned once a day, once a week, or maybe every weekend. Maybe we could even find time to pull out some stationery and scratch out a letter to Mom. Imagine how excited she'd be to know we took the time to stay connected the old-fashioned way.

Lord, please show me what's important and how to keep my focus on You. Thanks for blessing me in so many ways, and show me how I can keep in touch the old-fashioned way once in a while. Amen.

FORGET YOUR WORRIES

*Who of you by worrying can add
a single hour to your life?*
LUKE 12:25 NIV

Sometimes we spend too much time stressing about tomorrow. It's easy to see why. For many people, promoting worry has become their main purpose in life. Politicians try to terrify us about sky-is-falling budgets, nuclear power, climate change, the tight job market, and the list goes on and on. If we let ourselves, we could spend most of yesterday, much of today, and all of tomorrow biting our nails. This old problem, that new problem; there's no scarcity of issues to weigh us down. In truth, though, worrying won't help.

There are also the personal concerns: our height, frizzy hair (or hair loss), fluctuating weight, and relationships (or lack thereof). As humans, we all stew now and then. Sometimes our thoughts may grow dark with doubt as we wish that we were like that "other guy," the one with all the money, the nice convertible, or the one who appears to spend all day exercising. In other words, the competition.

The answer is to find something better to do

with our hands and minds. For example, when we are helping others, we aren't constantly thinking about ourselves and our woes. By taking ourselves out of the picture, we can spend a moment or two thinking and praying about all the little ones who go to bed hungry at night or don't have a blanket to pull up under their chins.

We should work on improving our habits and developing new skills. It may be a challenge, but we can do it. So get off the worry wagon. Move in the right direction, even if it's a hard, uphill journey. We can definitely do it if we try. Let's start today, right now.

Lord, please help me not to worry so easily.
Give me much-needed reminders of Your
faithfulness and constant love for me. Let me
keep in my heart the truth of Your goodness,
Your greatness, and Your power. Amen.

FOOD FEST

One of those at the table with Jesus heard these
things and said to him, "Blessed are the people
who will share in the meal in God's kingdom."
LUKE 14:15 NCV

Food, sweet or savory sustenance, is the source of
so many good times, good feelings, and even good
friends. Meeting for a meal or coffee is commonplace
because time at the table gives everyone a chance to
simply unwind and relax. No agenda, no demands.
And as a bonus, someone else gets to clean up when
we go out!

But when eating at Mom and Dad's diner, we
don't have to think about cleaning up, right? Of
course, maybe we should. But why stress? The
food's free, the table's set, and all we have to do is
unglue ourselves from the game console, TV, or
phone, and traipse into the dining room. It's a slight
inconvenience to unplug when we're in the middle
of creating a great text, but we're willing to make the
sacrifice for some home cooking!

Maybe we could also consider making a bit more
of a sacrifice and getting up *before* the meal's ready.

How about checking with Mom (or Dad) to see if there's anything we can help prep, throw out, or clean before dinner? Another great thought: we could hang around afterward to hand wash the sticky pots and pans. What a great time to catch up, talk about life, and maybe even open up about what's eating us.

It's easy to take a good thing for granted. We've all done it more than once (and some of us may do it many times a day). But let's take a second look. Even if we're just home for a visit, think about the source of all those good meals. And be sure to pitch in and help. Say thanks with not only words but a hug, too. It'll be greatly appreciated.

Lord, how quickly time passes. Please help me to see the needs in front of me and to be grateful for all the many ways You bestow Your good gifts. Thanks for the family and friends that feed my soul and the food that fills my stomach. Amen.

MOVING PAST MISTAKES

"If you do what is right, will you not be accepted?
But if you do not do what is right, sin is
crouching at your door; it desires to have you,
but you must rule over it."
<small>GENESIS 4:7 NIV</small>

If we really believe that we can get through a whole week or even an entire day without making a single mistake we probably need to reassess our grasp on reality! To think that mix-ups won't happen to us is to be hopeful beyond all reason.

Every week there is a myriad of small, annoying problems we may have to live with due to someone's carelessness or miscalculation (not necessarily our own). What's done can't be undone—only dealt with. We should discover what lessons can be learned from the inevitable mishaps and mangled misunderstandings that cloud our day.

When we've made a real mess of things, one approach is to simply hit REPLAY and torture ourselves by repeatedly reviewing the mistake, dwelling on how foolish we felt. Little is accomplished other than making ourselves feel bad or stupid.

Of course we shouldn't overlook the results and responsibilities of the things we do wrong, but a better approach is to face up to what's happened, ask for forgiveness, and move on.

Rather than ignoring deserved criticism or seeking a scapegoat, we should try the more mature method of dealing with the problem in a straightforward, helpful way. We shouldn't hide from the truth or waste time pretending it didn't happen. When there's time to reflect, we should make a list of what lessons can be gleaned and take that hard-earned experience with us for the next time a similar situation arises.

We certainly won't avoid all problems in the future this way, but we will have a whole new attitude about dealing with the difficulties in our lives. We *all* make mistakes. The big difference is that not everyone learns from them. Be the exception by dealing with the pain, accepting God's forgiveness, and moving ahead in hope.

Lord, I can't help seeing that horrible scene in my mind over and over. I know I must forgive myself and try to move on, but it's so difficult. Please give me Your comfort and hope. I really need it. Amen.

EVERYDAY ANSWERS

All humanity will come to You,
the One who hears prayer.
PSALM 65:2 HCSB

Seeking answers shows a desire to grow in both
knowledge and wisdom. As we move past graduation
day and into the future, it's only natural to continue
uncovering life's many secrets, both simple and
complex. But sometimes the universe doesn't easily
or willingly cough them up. No, the price we pay
for understanding (or attempting to understand)
can be high and very personal. We're like the latest
trailblazers on a journey traveled by many before us.

Of course, we're not alone. Our parents went
through the same bizarre otherworldly experience
of trying to forge a path for themselves. So did
their parents and so on. We need to keep this truth
in mind. Life can seem daunting and lonely when
we feel that we're the only ones facing pains and
troubles, doubts and questions.

For answers to our deepest spiritual longings,
the Bible is a great place to start. Learning from
our spiritual mentors is also valuable. But for the

everyday questions, there are numerous resources that can help us discover everything from how to tie a tie, make a seven-layer cake, detail a car, or stick with an exercise program.

No matter what type of information we seek, we must be wary of the source. With the Internet exploding with websites on virtually any topic imaginable, we can quickly locate the so-called bottom line. Before accepting the results of our search as authoritative, though, we've got to be sure that we haven't stumbled across someone trying to sell junk, steal information, or snatch our money. Check reviews and personal referrals, and always be hesitant about signing on to just anyone's mailing list. Let's use our smarts and only allow what's good, excellent, and worthy into our minds.

*Lord, help me to be honest with You about my many
questions. Help me to realize that I can come to You
with any and all concerns. And that You'll hear
and answer. . .no matter what. Amen.*

NO PLACE TO HIDE

*Anyone who lives on milk, being still an infant,
is not acquainted with the teaching
about righteousness.*
HEBREWS 5:13 NIV

We may think we're getting away with stuff, like looking at things, doing things, or saying things we wouldn't want anyone else to know about. But we are fooling ourselves. God knows everything, so we're not tricking Him. He hears our weak excuses when we venture down paths we should avoid. Through our years of schooling we may have seen people scam others, but there's absolutely no way to trick our Maker.

The next time we start slipping down a path that leads us from God's side, we must choose then and there to stop. If we don't give in, we won't go wrong. Now, before temptation strikes, we need to set boundaries and make sure they're strong well *before* the time of testing comes. Once temptation hits, we find out whether or not our promises were genuine or a joke.

When we were little we believed if we shut our

eyes and covered them with our hands, no one could see us. That was our logic when we played hide-and-seek. We'd snuggle down into the couch cushions and honestly think we were invisible. Our parents probably even played along. But now as we engage in more real-world excitement, we can no longer hold the juvenile idea that we can do whatever we want without being held to account. We're not children anymore and must now act like the adults we've become.

How do we stand firm in the face of temptation? By making the right choice from the start. However, when we do take a wrong turn, we must confess what we've done to those we've hurt and to God. We can then move on. We should never hide from the amazing gift of forgiveness. Neither should we try to keep the truth from God.

Oh God, please help me to be honest with You.
I know that You can see into my soul, and yet
sometimes I foolishly think I can trick You.
Help me to long to stay close by Your side.
I don't ever want to hide from You. Amen.

CLEAR YOUR SCHEDULE

*God said, "Let there be lights in the expanse
of the heavens to separate the day from the night,
and let them be for signs and for seasons
and for days and years."*
GENESIS 1:14 NASB

Calendars are worthwhile tools. Without them most
of us wouldn't make it to school, church, or the
movies on time. They come in all shapes and sizes
and will practically pinch us when we try to oversleep
or are close to missing an appointment. With every
opportunity to be on schedule, why is it that we often
still feel unfulfilled, exhausted, and overbooked?

Maybe it's because we become controlled by
our calendars and what others demand of us. Take
social networking sites, for example. Maybe instead
of trying to stay in touch with every person we know
every day, we should focus on a few devoted friends.
We should definitely stay close with those who care
deeply about us, our thoughts, and our dreams like
parents, spouses, siblings, and friends we made in
school. But if we spend all of our time online or cram
our day too full, we may miss the chance to go for a

walk and chat with the lonely man down the street.

How can we keep from getting choked by our to-do list? The quick answer is to schedule downtime into every day. We don't need to be on the go 24/7. Rather, we should find a few unhurried moments when we can be alone and think. Or pray or dream or wonder or question.

To do this will mean taking a breather from our calendar. We'll have to forget the computer, e-mail, and Facebook and take some time for ourselves. This exercise builds up our discipline and helps keep us focused on what is worth spending time on. Plan a break and discover some playtime—time to be free from everything tugging at us—in your day.

Lord, my life seems crazy busy all of the time.
Why can't I slow down? Please show me
some time I can reclaim to spend with
You and with those I love. Amen.

RICHEST OF THE RICH

Therefore do not worry about tomorrow,
for tomorrow will worry about itself.
MATTHEW 6:34 NIV

Today we hear about millionaires more than ever, and becoming a billionaire isn't as unusual as it once was. Every once in a while we may pause to consider how a massive infusion of cash could change our lives. Would we go on a spending spree or stuff it all under a mattress? Maybe we'd give most of it to the needy. It's hard to know for certain unless it happened.

Our whole perspective on friendship could change. We might keep our good fortune a secret, fearing others would want a relationship just for our money. This isn't a hypothetical concern for the wealthy. Sometimes they do become loners because they can't trust the motives of their supposed friends. Rather than enjoying relationships and the freedom wealth provides, they spend their time protecting their massive stockpiles. Money has become their closest companion.

On its face, there's nothing wrong with making money through honest, hard work. But if our only aim in life is to have a private jet, own expensive goodies, and live in luxury, we should reconsider our priorities. Money is just money. It comes and goes, and if it's more important than relationships with family or friends, those vital ties may unravel from lack of attention.

Certainly we should appreciate the monetary gifts God gives. But we can also find ways to enjoy what we have here and now (no matter how little that may be). Next time Christmas or a birthday rolls around, maybe we should consider a gift exchange with a friend where we have to make a gift. . .or find something at a thrift store. . .or spend no more than $5.00. Our creativity flourishes when we use our imagination instead of merely buying our way to fun.

Lord, please let me be thankful, whether I have great riches or am rich in love and friendship. Show me what's truly important each and every day. And, most of all, help me to put You first in my life and heart.
Amen.

THE DONE DEAL

*Forgive, and deal with everyone according
to all they do, since you know their hearts
(for you alone know the human heart).*
2 CHRONICLES 6:30 NIV

How good are we at the negotiating game? When
young, we all learned how to use a pathetic whimper
to ask for that extra sip of water. Or maybe a second
helping of dessert. Or perhaps a new pair of those
fancy shoes or jeans everyone had to have. With a
flash of our irresistible smile our moms or grandpas
became warm putty in our hands. Or at least that's
the way we remember it, right?

Why do some people always seem to get their
own way? Perhaps, in large part, it is because of their
long history of "playing nice with others." Think way
back to the early school-yard days. If there was a
new curvy slide, everyone wanted to have their turn.
To get to the top, we either shoved ahead or waited.
The pushy approach might have been effective
occasionally, but it certainly didn't make us many
long-term friends. In fact, when we shoved someone
they usually shoved back. It's the same way with life.

To get along, the best course is to take time to develop lasting connections with people. Listen to them, and show how much you care. That's how real relationships are built. Moment by moment and hour by hour. We can also deepen friendships by tearing up our long "gimme" list and giving in once in a while to what the other person needs.

When we open doors for others, our own opportunities often expand. Sure, we've heard that some claw their way to the top rung, but that's not how to sleep well at night. We've got to give to get, share to enjoy. And when making a deal or nurturing a relationship, let's take the time to be certain that both parties in the arrangement end up with something to smile about.

Oh God, help me to learn how to put the needs of others in a place of priority without allowing myself to be humiliated or run over. I want to be fair, but only as firm as necessary. Please help me to follow Your example. Amen.

SLOW PATIENCE

It is better to finish something than to start it.
It is better to be patient than to be proud.
ECCLESIASTES 7:8 NCV

Why is it so difficult to learn to be patient? Because it takes time, of course! If there were a way we could instantly move from banging on the piano keys to playing a concerto without any practice, we'd probably jump at the chance. We wouldn't have sore wrists and arms from running up and down boring scales. We'd move from super simple songs to Beethoven, Brahms, or Bach in minutes. Imagine sitting down and playing like a master. Unfortunately, it doesn't work that way in real life.

The truth is that we all develop patience in different ways, and for some it takes longer than others. Some of us can sit through a thousand-page book, watch a three-hour foreign film, train a puppy to go where he should, or make a perfect quiche at high altitude. God has gifted us in different ways, and those interests often guide our patience level.

Each of us has a different tolerance for the trivial, the menial, or the just plain time-consuming. From our experiences in school, we know there are some things we love to do that others find crazy-making. That's what makes us unique. It also means that we can expect our ability to build patience to increase in its own way and time.

For example, specific, focused effort like developing new skills can force us to develop more patience. Such changes may mean waking earlier or staying up later than we'd like (to write or study), or lifting heavy weights or taking long walks around the neighborhood (to improve our fitness). Each person will be challenged in different ways, depending on his or her goals. But one thing's certain, if we don't use our patience muscles, they'll never grow!

God, sometimes I fear that building up patience will
drive me crazy! I don't know what I'm supposed
to do while I work to develop it—except to wait.
But I do know that You are with me no matter what.
Help me to handle what I must. Amen.

THE DISTRACTION DILEMMA

Do you not know that in a race all the runners run,
but only one gets the prize? Run in such
a way as to get the prize.
1 CORINTHIANS 9:24 NIV

What's distracting us from completing what we start?
Back in school what kept us from studying like we
should have? A few examples might be video games,
TV, movies, web surfing, and social networking.
These aren't necessarily negative activities, but they
can keep us from completing our required goals.

Let's look at an everyday scenario. We start
working on an assignment and then realize we don't
have enough mechanical pencils. We go look for
them and think about how we haven't organized our
dresser in quite a while. So we pull out everything
from every drawer and dump it all in a heap. We start
sorting and folding. Whew. . . Some of the clothes
are dirty, some need to be donated, and some were
borrowed and need to be returned. One task becomes
many. Before long we need a break!

Later, after a warm meal, we watch TV. There's
that new show on. And then a text comes through and

we've got to jump onto our favorite blog or website. Soon, we've forgotten about the clothes and are ready for bed. So we carve a path to the mattress, leaving things a bigger mess than before.

Is there a way to solve the distraction dilemma? Yes! Come up with a short list of things that absolutely, positively have to be done. Shut off all distractions (phone, TV, computer). Put a timer on for forty-five focused minutes and then get to work. That's it for the day. Stop when the timer buzzes, and celebrate. We're forty-five minutes more finished than we have been in weeks. This is the simple secret to overcoming distractions. With some concentrated effort we can turn good intentions into results!

Lord, there are so many things that I must take care of. But it's not easy. I feel like I'm always tripping myself up. Please show me how I can focus on what's most important and deal with distractions in a healthy way. Amen.

REJOICE IN YOUR TRIUMPHS

*Saul said to David, "May you be blessed,
my son David! You shall both do great
things and also still prevail."*
1 Samuel 26:25 NKJV

Throughout school we had our share of victories, but now that we've graduated we realize that not all successes are created equal. Triumphs come in many shapes and sizes. A mountain of effort for one person barely works up a sweat in another. Some of us struggled to survive killer courses, while others made top grades without even trying. One lesson we should have learned is that it's pointless and unfair to compare ourselves with others. Everyone does things differently, and we don't always finish at the same time.

But when we succeed let's share the news. Those we care about will burst with pride and happiness to discover we've done what we set out to do. When we accomplish something important we should let everyone know so they can join in the fun. Going forward, keep in mind that one of the best parts of a win is the celebration! Shout for joy when we land a dream job, learn a new skill, or get the accolades we crave.

Whether the victory is little or large, our achievements are worthy of honor. God doesn't want us to hide our joy under a bushel. He wants us to be glad when we use the skills we've been blessed with. We should make special memories when we do something amazing. Like take pictures, have a little party, and blare out the news online.

When we're having a rough day let's look back at all we've already done with His help. Reviewing past successes underlines the truth that we can do far more than we think is possible. Look back over the last year and think about the one-of-a-kind things that were accomplished. The good stuff that makes us glow reminds us that we *can* tackle anything God has in store.

Lord, You are a God of amazing miracles.
You can do the impossible. Thanks for helping me
to accomplish big things—huge, amazing things—
that I never thought possible. Please let me use
my gifts for You and Your glory. Amen.

THE HARD TRUTH

The king said to him, "How many times must I make you swear to tell me nothing but the truth in the name of the LORD?"
1 KINGS 22:16 NIV

―――――

Truth's teeth can hurt, especially when they are chomping into our tender self-esteem. When it comes to singing a song, preparing a PowerPoint, or fixing a meal, we want to excel. In fact, it's beyond comprehension that we could possibly have failed to do what we set out to accomplish. What went wrong? Didn't we try our hardest, do our best, bring our "A" game? Maybe we did, but no one succeeds 100 percent of the time.

Picture any number of the contestants on various TV competitions, the ones who think they can sing, dance, or cook. They aren't all winners—that's for sure! Though maybe we're a bit uncomfortable, we can't help but smirk when the "judges" tell it like it is. From our vantage point on the couch we can clearly see that those people have talents that lie elsewhere.

So why in the world did they think that they could sing the stunning "Star-Spangled Banner" live before millions? We cover our ears groaning. Or giggling. Why did they make a fool of themselves? Because they never heard the truth. They never received (or believed) the hard news that they should try something else.

It takes a brave heart to listen to someone critique us. For such honesty to be effective, we can't get our back up or whine or complain about the unfairness of it all. We might even learn something if we accept that we have room for improvement. It's perfectly fine to sing off-key if we love to belt out a tune in the shower. Have at it! But we shouldn't fool ourselves into thinking we're gifted in ways we're not. Let's find our true talents and allow them to take us to the stars!

Lord, I know You've given me many gifts. Please help me see those that are hidden, use those that are obvious, and enjoy the talents of others in areas where I fall short. Thanks for making us all so amazingly different. Amen.

FREE RIDE

*"I will sacrifice to You with the voice of thanksgiving.
That which I have vowed I will pay.
Salvation is from the LORD."*
JONAH 2:9 NASB

Imagine sitting around all day, every day, playing games, talking with friends, eating whatever we want, and never cleaning up after ourselves. Dream come true or mind-numbing boredom? One reason we may like the idea of not having to work is our curiosity about living far above the everyday hassles of life. Without lifting a finger, we could have everything we've ever wanted. So could all our friends!

There's a catch though. If we don't personally sacrifice and work hard for something, it's not as valuable to us. That's why many who inherit wealth or win the lottery end up squandering their cash. They didn't earn it and have no grasp on the true value of all the money they let slip through their fingers.

When we lived at home we barely noticed the sacrifice that our parents expended to give us what we needed. We just held out our hands and took all we could hold. The opportunity to get stuff free and take advantage of those who work hard is a real temptation. However, once we start paying our own bills, filing our own taxes, and covering rent, meals, gasoline, and utilities, we quickly see that in the real world every penny needs to be counted.

Let's promise right now to start saving for the things that matter and resist the temptation to pull out a credit card. That gives us the false sense that we have unlimited funds. Actually, by borrowing now we're cutting into our future spending opportunities. And no matter how long we stretch out payments, eventually we will have to pay—with interest. The less we owe, though, the smaller our bill will be when the day of reckoning comes.

Lord, You give me so much so often, and yet I never feel completely satisfied. There's always one more thing I've got to have. One more want. Please show me how to be grateful and not grasping. Amen.

WHAT DOES "GREAT" MEAN?

*They will live securely, for then his greatness
will reach to the ends of the earth.*

MICAH 5:4 NIV

Ask ten different people and we'd get ten different
answers about the meaning of greatness. We all
picture something different. But if we can't come to
some agreement about the definition of the word,
then how do we know when someone has arrived at
the exalted state of "great"?

Society sees greatness in powerful people who
have lots of money and influence. In those who can
do *as* they please, *when* they please. If we tried to
explain what makes us, our families, our state or
country great, we'd be surprised at the variety of
answers. Perhaps it's also possible that what was
once great no longer is. That's because nothing stays
constant—except God. Greatness, then, isn't static.
The status of "being great," whether we're talking
about a school's team, a restaurant, or the president,
shifts with time and polls. To retain such an accolade,
one must keep striving to retain it.

Many questions could be asked in determining

a person's Greatness Factor. Does being great mean that we can do anything—or that we have the heart to sacrifice our time for others? Do we lead by serving, or do we define greatness by the number of people we can boss around?

When it comes to a spiritual definition, being great means being willing to give of ourselves without expecting something in return. Making sacrifices without expecting a response or a reward. Helping out around the house or at the job site without demanding tangible rewards. It means stepping out of the limelight and exalting others. Listening when a friend needs help. All of these approaches give us glimpses of greatness. Not the greatness of monuments and statues, but the greatness of spirit and heart. A humble magnificence that pleases God.

Lord, please show me how I may become a great servant of God. I want to learn what it means to give of myself without demanding the praise of others. Help me to long for Your praise alone. Amen.

ENCOURAGEMENT

Brothers and sisters, rejoice! Strive for full restoration,
encourage one another, be of one mind, live in peace.
And the God of love and peace will be with you.
2 Corinthians 13:11 niv

Negativity comes easy. It's a breeze to pick on
someone's behavioral flaws, clothing mistakes, and
personality problems. Such conduct is modeled all
the time. When we were children, the existence of
cliques was felt most at recess. The "in" and "out"
crowds were glaringly obvious. And everyone who's
been at the receiving end of a barb knows that
words can hurt. The media today encourages these
pointless feuds because they raise viewer ratings.
Two people go after each other claiming they're
telling the "truth." Instead, though, they only want to
tear open old wounds and cause maximal pain.

Let's try to look for—and up to—people who use
words to encourage others, not shred the tenderhearted
to the point of tears. What makes such comments
sting? One thing is that we often feel defenseless
against nasty remarks from out of the blue. Our
clever comebacks usually come to us far too late.

We often find ourselves hungry for hope and encouragement. Maybe it's been far too long since someone said "I love you," called us special, or complimented our gifts and talents. When we hang around with the negative, nitpicking crowd, our hearts become downtrodden. Our minds get stuck in ruts. We should instead seek out influencers who can make us smile.

Even if our day is one mess after another, we can still encourage someone else. Maybe not even a person we know. At the bank we can thank the teller for helping us. When we comment on someone's great smile or kind eyes, it's a guarantee that we've made their day. Make a promise to dole out compliments generously. We should enjoy saying kind things as much as we like hearing them. Encouragement is contagious—spread some today.

Lord, I know it takes only a few simple little words to make someone else's day. Let me be the person who uplifts and encourages. Give me the grace to show appreciation to others. Amen.

SMALL GIFTS

The LORD brings poverty and gives wealth;
He humbles and He exalts.
1 SAMUEL 2:7 HCSB

Giving little presents brings joy to the recipient—and the giver. Remember how much a small token of love meant when we were struggling in school? Such kindness can be inexpensive and still go a long way toward making someone smile.

We've got to keep our ears open when someone mentions a favorite book, song, or movie. Maybe we can find a sale on a hot music download or a cool movie tie-in. There are lots of them, especially with so many big theatrical releases each week. Grocery stores and convenience marts often carry special movie tie-in promotions that a friend might love if he or she is a huge fan of the film. So slurp down a few colas and give that friend a four-piece drinking glass set!

At thrift or secondhand stores, we can keep our eyes open for potential perfect gifts—presents that show we're thinking of those we care about. It all starts with knowing what moves the people in our lives. This means we have to actually listen to them and take note of what they're saying. Keeping a list is a good idea!

That's really what this is all about: making someone else happy. It's about putting another person's interests and desires above our own. Once we begin collecting these treasures, we can keep a small cache of special little presents. Include favorites like a clearance gourmet candy bar or two, attractive discounted books or cards, or maybe scarves, jewelry, or letter openers.

These "just because" presents allow us to play the role of random gift giver whenever we'd like. Nothing extravagant or fancy, just a few items that can be given to say "you're special" or "I care about you." No pressure, no demands, no expectations, just a tiny bit of kindness. . .straight from the heart.

Lord, every day You give me opportunities to help others. Sometimes people need a little extra something to show them I care. Please show me how I can tangibly give of myself and my possessions to encourage someone. Amen.

DEATH'S SHARP STING

"Where, O death, is your victory?
Where, O death, is your sting?"
1 Corinthians 15:55 niv

Once we've experienced the loss of a loved one we understand all too vividly the grief and sadness that come with such a tragedy. A single death can make a tremendous difference in our lives, sapping us of joy and strength, especially if it's someone precious, a person we've known for years like a beloved grandfather, for example. Through the years we'd built memories with and around him. We'd done things together, made silly jokes, and visited great places. He held us and hugged us ever since we were tiny.

We hoped that somehow this sad day might never come. But then Grandpa got sick, and then got worse. Soon nothing could be done but send cards and pray. We may have gone to the funeral or memorial service. Or maybe we lived far away and couldn't afford the trip. A death like that leaves a confused place in the heart. Anger even. How could death be so cruel as to take away someone we loved?

But that's exactly the point. Death kills. It

destroys. It separates family and friends. It hurts and shocks us. We weep when we think about that warm smile, the love, and the companionship. We miss Gramps.

Fortunately, those bound together by faith will see each other again one day. Heaven is a beautiful place, full of vistas and mountaintops, more incredible than we can imagine. It's a place of life and health, not infected with darkness, death, and despair. Heaven promises that someday we'll again enjoy being in the presence of those we've lost. Not only will we see God's shining face, but we'll get to walk and talk with those who meant so much to us—and love us still.

God, sometimes it hurts to love someone,
especially when I see that person hurting and in pain.
Thanks for bringing sweet memories to my mind
and helping me remember the good times
I had with those I miss so much. Amen.

ASKING FOR HELP

*"Let my teaching drop as the rain, my speech
distill as the dew, as the droplets on the fresh
grass and as the showers on the herb."*
DEUTERONOMY 32:2 NASB

One sign of maturity is knowing when to ask for help.
Few people are willing to do this. Somehow it seems
easier to try figuring things out than to ask questions.
That's because the ultimate mortification in society
is looking foolish or acting like we don't know
something. However, that cool veneer flakes off when
we don't know what we're talking about.

We can short-circuit such worries by continually
seeking opportunities to learn. We know from our
educational experiences that different people grasp
information in different ways. Some like to see the
lesson, others hear it, and still others find that reading
about a topic is most effective. Knowing how we best
learn is also important. The secret to assimilating
new knowledge is to follow this basic pattern: learn
about a new skill in the manner most appropriate to
your study style, and then do the skill personally.

We should take our time and keep at it until we

get comfortable. Finally, we need to teach someone else the skill. This builds a mind-body connection and embeds the details into both our heads and hands.

No matter what others may model, we should never be afraid to admit we have a lot to learn. Until we get the assistance we need, we might never discover a fresh inclination or talent.

Let's remember that it doesn't make us foolish to ask questions or seek an explanation. Instead, what is silly is to fail to ask for help, especially when there's a ready and willing educator nearby. Whether that teacher is a parent, friend, or neighbor, we've all got much to learn. And we can—if only we'll humble ourselves and exhibit a sincere desire to grow.

God, there are many times that I'm afraid to admit how much I don't know. Please give me the courage to ask others for help. And remind me that it's okay to keep learning at any stage of life. Amen.

HUMOR

*Blessed are you who hunger now, for you
will be satisfied. Blessed are you who
weep now, for you will laugh.*
LUKE 6:21 NIV

Everything that people laugh at isn't always
humorous. Far from it. We've all seen shared videos
and thought, *What in the world makes people think
this is funny?* Sick humor pervades the media,
movies, books, TV, and magazines. Many performers
choose the low road when it comes to amusing
their audiences. Instead of making us think, they do
something disgusting or tell a dirty joke and expect
a laugh.

Of course, to recognize something as funny
we've got to have a sense of humor. That means
being willing to giggle or guffaw even if we get some
strange stares. Only the very bravest are willing
to laugh at themselves. We all do things that are
amusing and embarrassing. If we act arrogant, we
better watch out! Pride (and lots of loud laughter
from everyone watching) always comes before a fall.
Certainly we need a serious side, but let's never be

afraid to see the humor in a situation.

Sad events go on in our world every day. Laughter eases the tension and lets us forget our worries for a while. There's nothing wrong with that. Chortling over an amusing (read: not mean) practical joke can be fun, too. There is funny. . .and then there is hurtful. Hold back on sawing away at a person's branch of self-esteem. Although we might get some cheap laughs by tearing someone else down, we should avoid such opportunities.

Find genuine humor in spontaneous silly situations. But avoid making fun of people, especially for things they can't help or don't even realize. We have to admit we're glad when someone shows us that same mercy. Our time on earth is short. When we laugh heartily with a friend, we can make it just a bit sweeter.

Lord, I think sometimes I spend too much time feeling sad. Help me to overlook the negative reports and find some of the good news that's happening all around us every day. Please give me something to make me smile—and laugh about—as well. Amen.

MONEY, MONEY, MONEY

Don't worry about the food or drink you need to live, or about the clothes you need for your body. Life is more than food, and the body is more than clothes.
MATTHEW 6:25 NCV

As we compete in the real world in real time our priorities become more apparent. Without doubt, pocketfuls of cash make a person stand out. Some even show off their wealth by ostentatiously displaying fancy clothes, cars, toys, and accessories. Individuals can quickly become newsmakers by spending outrageous prices for shoes, a purse, or an island paradise.

Though maybe our first response might be to scoff at such extravagance, deep down we wish for a whiff of that lavish lifestyle. Perhaps that's because the scales don't always seem quite balanced. While we should be satisfied with the good gifts we have (many of which are stuffed in the closet, garage, or car), at times we feel tempted by all the enticing advertisements.

But there is an easy way to avoid envy. Make a list of every blessing. Think of the opportunities we've been given, the joys experienced, and the places explored. Look at nature's amazing display just outside the window, and consider the gifts of sight, hearing, and our other senses. Rejoice in the simple fact that we can run, skip, jump, and dance (hopefully) without pain. We can't put a price on these intangibles unless it's to remind ourselves of how positively spoiled we are.

Here's another exercise. Keep track of all spending for a month. This record shows what's important to us. If we're willing to buy it, then it must be a necessity, right? Flipping through a checkbook or credit card statement shows exactly what our top priorities are. Don't treat shopping like a sport. Keep essentials priority, and save the rest of your hard-earned money. We know that's not easy! But if we can conquer the challenge of living within our means, we'll find a priceless contentment that few can claim.

God, forgive me when I become a glutton
for worldly things. Help me not to be greedy
for things that don't matter in the long run.
Instead, help me to be hungry for true life and
spiritual strength that only You can give. Amen.

GOD FORGIVES SIN

Who is a God like you, who pardons sin
and forgives the transgression of the remnant
of his inheritance? You do not stay angry
forever but delight to show mercy.
MICAH 7:18 NIV

Reaching the graduation milestone doesn't mean
we won't make any more mistakes. Everyone is
occasionally guilty of horrible timing and a shocking
lack of planning. At times we neglect common sense
and run out of gas on the freeway. Or forget to say
"thank you" or "I'm sorry" and wind up hurting
someone's feelings.

But at other times we blow it big. We do what
we know we shouldn't. In our darkest moments
we realize what has happened and reflect on our
foolishness. Nothing will hide the fact that we've
willfully chosen the wrong course of action, knowing
exactly what we were doing. People sin constantly,
though even mentioning iniquity is unpopular in
today's politically correct world.

Once the deed is done, we have choices. Hide the
truth or confess to God. The decision can be difficult.

Imagine if others could hear our hidden thoughts or probe what's buried in our hearts. What if all that gunk was suddenly made public? What would we do? Where would we hide? Sometimes, despite our maturity, we act in mean, hurtful ways. We displease God, friends, family, and ourselves with our anger. We've all done things we never want to be reminded of.

Thankfully, there's an amazing, undeserved gift called forgiveness. Big or small, our mistakes don't have to stay glued to our souls forever if we're truly sorry, if we ask for forgiveness, and if we genuinely turn from our sins. It's a miracle, but one that we can access whenever we want to wash our hands and hearts of the bad stuff—and make a fresh start. Maybe we're still trying to hide the hard truth from an all-seeing, all-knowing God. Now's the time to check in with Him, unburden ourselves, and feel the amazing power of His forgiveness.

Oh God, sometimes I really blow it.
I know exactly what I shouldn't do and yet
do it anyway. Please help me to come to You
for forgiveness when I choose wrong over right.
Thanks for letting me start fresh whenever I ask.
Amen.

GOD BLESS AMERICA

*Blessed is the nation whose God is the LORD, the
people He has chosen as His own inheritance.*
PSALM 33:12 NKJV

Thanks to our fantastic First Amendment freedoms,
many detractors seem bent on finding an angle to
slam the U.S. of A. But when we take an honest look
at America we see a massive quilt of accomplishment
and sacrifice that covers us and binds us together.

America is, after all, a place many want to live—
mostly because of the numerous freedoms we enjoy.
We can speak our minds, worship as we choose,
pursue happiness, even run for president. A trip
across this country allows us to meet creative and
amazing people and see some of the most varied and
stunning landscapes imaginable.

Sure, America's not perfect, but when anyone,
anywhere around the world, suffers a disaster,
American volunteers and representatives are among
the first to board the planes and ships to bring
comfort and relief. We give food, clothing, medicine,
and help to those in need around the world. And
when horror visits us here, first responders like

nurses, firefighters, EMTs, and doctors run straight toward the danger ready to do anything possible to help others.

We should always be proud of the things that make this nation one-of-a-kind, taking time to reflect on why millions seek to make this land of the free and home of the brave their home, too. She's a beautiful, generous, bountiful land. Let's be honest and balanced when speaking her name. And as Americans, we should realize that when we all come together great things can happen.

Lord, I am blessed to call this nation mine.
Please show me ways that I can pray for this country,
our leaders, and those who would harm us.
Thank You for giving me a place where I can
live and worship in freedom. Amen.

THE ENEMY NEVER SLEEPS

*Be alert and of sober mind. Your enemy the devil
prowls around like a roaring lion looking
for someone to devour.*
1 PETER 5:8 NIV

We must be wary because Satan is on the prowl. The devil? Really? Isn't he that harmless little guy in the dark red suit poking people with a plastic pitchfork? Indeed, that's how we've been conditioned to think of the enemy of our souls. We don't like the idea that there could really be someone dangerous out to get us. Someone full of hate who doesn't want us to experience the peace and joy that is only available through a close connection to God.

Truth is, the Almighty has many enemies. Spiritually, when we decide to serve God a target is plastered on our backs. Don't think for a second that being a believer assures us of good times and easy living. Sometimes just the opposite is true. When we decide (or make the decision one day) to accept God's sacrificial gift of His Son we enter a whole new realm of reality. Suddenly, our spiritual blinders are thrown aside and we have a glimpse of the world as

God sees it. A dark side of sin and rebellion—and His side. Two forces battling for every soul.

This is serious. We don't have the luxury of resting on the work done by others. Same as when we were in school. We may have been a part of a study group or done projects together with friends, but ultimately it was how we did on the test and our personal GPA that mattered most. And we didn't have anyone to blame except ourselves if the grades didn't match our goals.

The same goes for our spiritual walk. The Enemy wants to yank us away from God and laugh as we fall and fail. But he can't if we consistently seek God's strength and support.

God, please let me stand firm for the truth that You are God. I know that temptations come often—and I've got to be ready. Thanks for saving me from a life of darkness and sin. I love You. Amen.

GETTING TO OUR GOALS

May the God of peace Himself sanctify you entirely;
and may your spirit and soul and body be
preserved complete, without blame at
the coming of our Lord Jesus Christ.
1 Thessalonians 5:23 nasb

When it comes to accomplishing things, we do what needs to be done. We know what it takes to pass a course or come out on top in the class ranking. Though short-term and long-term desires differ for each of us, ultimately we all want some version of the following: a good job that pays the bills, a chance to help others, and an opportunity to stretch our minds and our options.

Throughout our educational journey, certain moments would undoubtedly come when we felt free to learn. There were times when it all clicked simultaneously. We understood things we've never known before. It can still make us smile to think of those golden instances when, after some struggle, we finally said, "Yeah, I get that!"

But to be honest, those pleasant plateaus of pure learning may have been fairly infrequent. That's because most of the time we struggled mightily against distractions like feeling tired or hungry or just wanting to get outside and do something else (anything else!). Instead of studying, perhaps we spent time thinking, complaining, exploring our feelings, and maybe even enjoying the company of our fellow students. Though we need to break up the monotony, we still must prepare to meet our goals.

So it is with our spiritual life. We must work to stay close to God. Read the Word, pray regularly, get involved in studies, and selflessly volunteer. But we can become so overwhelmed trying to do all the right things that we forget to soften our hearts to absorb the truth. We are so overcome with to-do lists and details that we forget to open our ears and listen. We must beware of our many self-imposed rules and requirements. Recognize them for what they are, and strive to stay focused on what's truly important.

Lord, I'm sorry when I make all the right motions and still come up short. Help me to see those times when I'm fooling myself. Let me learn with the right motives and grow in ways that allow me to serve You better. Amen.

LOOKING FOR PROOF

*After his suffering, he presented himself to them
and gave many convincing proofs that he was alive.
He appeared to them over a period of forty days
and spoke about the kingdom of God.*
ACTS 1:3 NIV

Does anyone take anything for granted anymore?
With all of the digital magic and manipulation at the
fingertips of the savvy user, it's no longer possible
to always believe our own eyes. From the biggest
decision to the smallest detail, people want to see
the hard evidence. And that's actually good. Don't
just take someone's word for it. Get the proof, test the
theory.

Perhaps it's all the criminal investigation shows
that we watch, but many of us have become amateur
detectives. Throughout our school years, we've been
taught never to simply accept things by faith but
instead to test what we know or think we know, to try
to figure out if we believe what's true or are falling for
a trick.

There are, of course, multiple ways to view the
results of any inquiry. The details are often at issue

or confused. And even when a "professional" makes the determination that "this is what really happened," there is always another side, another point of view. We may think that the experts have all the answers, but they're guessing, too. Just because someone is completely competent doesn't mean they're necessarily right.

From our varied life experiences, we should look at the source of information coming our way. This is often an excellent guide to knowing whether or not we should believe the supposed proof before our eyes. For example, we know that God's Word is the source of truth. If it is being mocked, challenged, or ignored, we need to carefully consider who's trying to sell us on their negative perspective. Remember, one person's biased opinion is not proof. But countless changed lives following a commitment to God and His Word? Now that is proof we can believe in.

God, please help me be a testimony to Your truth.
Even though I make mistakes I still love You
and believe in You. Take away my doubts,
and let me know that You are and shall
always be the source of all truth. Amen.

REST IN HIM

They spoke to the LORD's angel, who was
standing among the myrtle trees. They said,
"We have gone through all the earth,
and everything is calm and quiet."
ZECHARIAH 1:11 NCV

What prompts that vague feeling that somehow we're getting behind everyone else? This sensation hits us every morning when we first flick on our phone, the radio, or TV. We're hungry for news! What's going on in the world, and what should our response be? Should we be doing more, getting more involved somehow?

The challenge to accomplish bigger and better things also hits us at a professional level. Are we living up to our potential? With all that schooling behind us and the expenses looming ahead, are we doing everything possible to succeed? Making the most of our opportunities? When we're at work we often feel pressured to attend more meetings, take on more responsibilities, and do more with less, as the saying goes. If we don't, we're accused of slacking off. Even in our personal lives we can feel the pressure to exercise more, read more, and travel more. More, more, more.

All of our activities may seem to give us a sense of value and worth. If we keep busy enough, perhaps we'll be able to overlook the emptiness within. This may be why we constantly push to excel, to be on top. Such endless activity prevents us from having to handle difficult questions or think through tough issues.

Maybe we need to give it a rest sometimes. Just push the pause button. Turn off our revving thoughts and simply read the Word and pray. Let's stop whirling around at the crazy pace the world demands. Just rest in Him once in a while. We can do it but only if we're willing to take a breather. Let's wait on Him rather than rushing to meet our own self-imposed deadlines.

Lord, please help me know when You're calling me to peace and quiet. Sometimes it takes illness to slow me down. Help me to rest in You, pray, and be more in tune to what's best for me and my spiritual health. Amen.

RECOGNIZE HIS GIFTS

Each one should test their own actions. Then they can take pride in themselves alone, without comparing themselves to someone else.
GALATIANS 6:4 NIV

We have seen them occasionally during our educational journey—those exceptional people who stand out because of their unique skills. Be it sports, writing, math, or science, there are numerous gifted individuals who amaze us with their energy, entrepreneurial spirit, and practical smarts. When we discover such stories of success, our initial thought may be to wonder why such super achievement couldn't be ours. How could someone else make such tremendous progress when we feel as though we're spinning our wheels? Not moving ahead, simply struggling to stay right where we are.

Hopefully, though, when we hear of an amazing accomplishment our next response is to send best wishes and warm thoughts to that person for their achievement or to commend them for helping others with the new product or process they've designed. That's what's so powerful about online communication tools. In this small world, we may personally know someone like this. But even if we don't, we should encourage those inventive people who strive to accomplish big things. Their results benefit us, benefit everyone! In some cases, the difference between life and death depends on using their new techniques or tools.

How incredible to share in someone else's success story. Think of it. Through prayer and online commendations, we have instant opportunities to encourage these movers and shakers, especially those within our own sphere of influence. Let's reach out to the high achiever. And when we can mentor a younger talent toward success we should willingly do so. Even if we're not the one in the spotlight we can still do great things—and have a small part in amazing achievements—by offering our gifts of prayer and encouragement.

Lord, sometimes I feel threatened by someone with tremendous talent. I worry that my own flame will seem not to burn as bright by comparison. Instead, help me to enjoy the gifts given to others and share my own freely. Amen.

PRAYER POWER

The Lord said to him: "I have heard your prayer and your supplication that you have made before Me."
I Kings 9:3 NKJV

Throughout the years we've seen prayer modeled in many ways, like those said at church services, meals, or by the bedside at night. All are excellent opportunities to set aside focused time to deal with the day's concerns. Designating a regular time to talk to God is a good practice, but it takes discipline. Like many other good habits, it can be neglected if we don't make it a priority. As we continually get busier, prayer should become an intricate piece in the pattern of our lives.

Not everyone grew up believing in the power of prayer. To some, the idea of talking to God is strange and uncomfortable. They may think of prayer as a formulaic approach heard only at official religious ceremonies and special services. That's a common view, especially when they hear unusual, "churchy-sounding" words. Those who pray infrequently typically only utter words to God out of desperation and fear. While He certainly does hear us even through our fear and despair, we needn't reserve our conversations with Him to those times when things are falling apart.

Prayer is a chance to unload many and varied reflections and worries. We can ask anything we want and even express anger and hurt. And we can hope and dream through the prayers we offer. Nothing's off-limits when we sit, stand, walk, or kneel before God. He will hear our deepest longings and petty concerns if we'll make our needs known.

The Almighty takes the time to listen to each of us, remember our names, and provide comfort and help. When we pray, the world opens up and our worries melt away. Let's accept His help and take advantage of a life-changing opportunity to chat with the Creator.

God, thanks for hearing my prayer.
Thanks for listening to each small detail and
concern that I bring to You. Please help me to have
an open heart to learn what I must and hear what
I need to so that I can serve You better. Amen.

PACKING FOR THE FIRE

Where your treasure is, there your heart will be also.
MATTHEW 6:21 NIV

If we were turtles and carried our homes on our backs there wouldn't be room for all the extras that currently weigh us down. We couldn't take along closets full of clothes, boxes of books, or our big-screen TV, because none of it would fit. But since we aren't limited by a shell, we can fill up entire houses and then spill over into the space in the garage, attic, or storage unit. Eventually, though, we'll need to trim back on the mounds of stuff we've accumulated.

Granted, some of the things we've saved are invaluable. There are old school projects, faded toys and games, and well-worn books we once treasured. Should we throw everything in a Dumpster or haul it to the thrift store? Of course not. One day we might have a little boy or girl of our own who will want to cuddle our best stuffed animal or favorite blanket. Unfortunately, though, it's impossible to save everything.

We must decide what's important. If old books and photos don't mean much to us, then we should

see if a sibling, parent, or relative would like them.
Our sense of what's valuable can change at times.
One day we can't wait to get rid of whatever it is that
weighs us down and the next we're upset because
we've lost a one-of-a-kind comic book or video.

We should keep the things that are truly
irreplaceable. Letters, cards, and notes that mean the
world to us, for example. But we must answer the big
question: If we could only save one box from a raging
fire, what would it contain? That tells us what's truly
priceless and what we should hang on to, no matter
what.

God, please help me see what truly matters.
Help me write Your words on my heart. Help me make
memories that mean something and that are truly
worth saving as I seek to strengthen relationships,
encourage friendships, and draw nearer to You. Amen.

WHERE'S YOUR WELL?

*We remember before our God and Father
your work produced by faith, your labor prompted
by love, and your endurance inspired
by hope in our Lord Jesus Christ.*
1 THESSALONIANS 1:3 NIV

Deep within us springs the desire to do amazing
things. Discoveries await us but only if we make time
to do what we're driven to do—what we're inspired to
do. Things like write a book or compose a concerto or
make the movies we imagine in our mind. Sometimes
a dream will give us an idea that moves and
motivates us. Other times, it is the word of a friend or
the encouragement of a mentor that causes our fount
of creativity to flow.

The source of inspiration varies from person to
person. Rarely do we feel fulfilled simply by copying
the work of others. Though this approach can help
strengthen basic technique in painting, for example,
we all seem to most enjoy finding our own ways of
seeing and doing things. Excellent, unique work may
require us to go in our own direction. At times, input
from others may be discouraging. When someone

tells us we're off track, let's listen politely but stick with whatever approach God has given us.

We may find that a certain setup of computer equipment or a special desk allows greater inventiveness. Our physical surroundings do matter. We should keep ideas that work but be willing to make changes if we find our inspiration becoming sluggish. Creativity is individual to each of us—and may be found in people, places, pets, and plants. Each such source hides glimpses of God if we'll take a moment to look. He has made many unique visions and shades of His glory.

God's world contains beauty beyond compare. So should ours. Let's put up a beautiful photo, framed Bible verse, or profound artwork. Such displays increase our chances of finding inspiration and triggering connections with the Creator.

God, let me see the amazing beauty in Your creation,
in those You've created, and in my own mind and
heart. Help me to build new opportunities, discover
new things, and learn new ways to help others. Amen.

THE SECRET

Encourage each other with these words.
1 THESSALONIANS 4:18 NCV

Person-to-person connections make the world go round. How we address others, act around others, and treat others often reveals whether or not we know the secret to good relationships: kindness, openness, honesty, and sincerity. We wouldn't ask a stranger for a favor. What right do we have to impose? Yet we do something similar when we ask Mom for the keys or a friend for a loan when we haven't communicated with either of them beyond an occasional "hey" or "later."

No one likes to feel used or taken for granted. We've all had painful moments when someone practically demanded we do something for them. Not because they cared about us or even asked politely, but because it's what they wanted at that moment. Being treated like the hired help hurts. Such a person has no rights or say. That's how we can come across when we force favors without first showing honest appreciation. Perhaps there are some close connections with parents, siblings, grandparents, or friends that we need to mend even now.

Simple words of kindness are easy. "I appreciate you," "I'm thankful for you," and "I want to know what you think" all work nicely. And don't forget "I love you," accompanied by a warm hug, as appropriate. Concentrate on the person, looking him or her in the eye. Communication isn't hard, but it does take time, focus, and practice. Not all of us have the ability to talk to anyone, anytime, about anything. But we can start improving that skill today by saying the little things that bring joy to others. Best of all, we're very likely to be pleased by the pleasant response.

God, I know I miss opportunities every day to
encourage others and tell them what they mean to me.
Help me say the right words at the right time.
I thank You for the many ways You uplift me.
Help me to do the same for others. Amen.

SEE THE NEED

*Is it not to share your food with the hungry and
to provide the poor wanderer with shelter—when
you see the naked, to clothe them, and not to
turn away from your own flesh and blood?*
ISAIAH 58:7 NIV

The world is full of needy people, like children who
go to bed hungry with little hope for tomorrow.
Maybe we're too isolated to see this pain. Do we know
how the less fortunate in our community—or the
world—eke out an existence? If the only things that
matter to us are found within the narrow boundaries
of familiarity, we need to expand our horizons. How
can we hope to understand or even empathize with
others when we don't know the first thing about
them? It's not enough to try ethnic food or watch
foreign films. We should make opportunities to meet
people from other cultures—people who don't think
or do things the way we do.

Chances are that few of us know where the "bad
parts" of town are, let alone make it a point to visit
them. Safety and security are important, but they
shouldn't be our only priorities. When we ignore the

rough spots of reality around us, we don't learn how to help those whose needs differ from our own.

Let's take stock of our own cultural awareness level. When looking at our community, how many foreign-language churches and businesses can we count? Opportunities exist to get to know people who aren't from around here. With a little effort, we can open our eyes to those struggling in the shadows. We can see what local churches, food kitchens, and outreaches are doing to help newcomers feel welcome in our country. Maybe we can look through our personal stockpile of shoes, clothes, and coats and donate some of the excess to those who don't have enough. The poor and homeless are always with us. It's up to us to see their needs and reach out to them in practical, caring ways.

Lord, let me be a light to others. Give me opportunities to reach out to those in need, especially those who are from other lands. Thanks for showing grace to me, and help me to share Your compassion with others. Amen.

SHORT STORY

Children's children are a crown to the aged,
and parents are the pride of their children.
PROVERBS 17:6 NIV

Time passes quickly. Just ask the older generation.
But right now, who has time to worry about the
future? We've got too much to do. As life progresses,
new opportunities for busyness continually present
themselves. Travel, marriage, children, and then,
one day, maybe even grandchildren. A life spent
surrounded by beloved family and friends is a
blessing beyond measure.

We don't know how it will feel, though—the
whole aging thing. Sometimes the unknown makes
us nervous. What will it be like to feel more tired,
regularly ache, hear our joints creak, or see our
hair fade and whiten? The good news is that those
changes aren't worth highlighting, because we'll be
able to handle them. We don't have to get stressed
about the number of candles on a cake.

Of course, there's no reason to rush things. Soon
enough our mirror will reveal young eyes trapped in a
lined face. One day in the future, we will enter

our twilight or golden years. Really that's just a slice of time when we can actually do what we want and enjoy spending time with our loved ones. Hopefully, it works out that way, but sometimes unfortunate circumstances and changes in our health prevent us from making the most of the time remaining.

We never know when heaven may call us. So let's take advantage of our opportunities now, no matter what our age. We can do what we love, live honestly, and avoid lingering regrets. One day when we tell the story of our lives, we'll look at images from the past, amazed at how close we are to the finish line. We shouldn't be afraid to grow up, grow old, and grow in God's grace, especially if we live each day with joy and expectancy.

Lord, I know that sometimes it seems that the days crawl by, but from Your perspective I must be running through my life. Help me to press PAUSE often and just enjoy the sweet moments You give me. Amen.

PLAY WITH THE RECIPE

When he had brought them into his house,
he set food before them; and he rejoiced,
having believed in God with all his household.
ACTS 16:34 NKJV

———————

There are two categories of people: those who like
to cook and those who like to eat. Sometimes they
even overlap! One thing we all know for certain
is that a recipe can be vital when making certain
foods, especially for the first time. Like brownies,
for example. We might have a vague idea about
what's in that delicacy, but we can't know for sure
unless we check before pulling out the mixing bowl.
The recipe serves as a safety net. It promises that if
we pay attention and check the oven temperature,
ingredient amounts, and cooking time, we'll have
success. Of course, fine-tuning is required. If we live
in the mountains, certain adjustments are required to
assure that the treats turn out.

Once we master Brownie Basics 101, we can start
experimenting. We can double recipes, triple them,
half them, maybe even share them! To make them
gooier and more like fudge, we simply slide them out

of the oven early. To make them extra rich, we dump in more chocolate chips or different combinations of chips. Or we may goop in swirls of marshmallow or caramel. Depending on personal preferences, we might add nuts, coconut, or chopped dried cherries. There are even certain suspicious bakers who put in stuff that's good for us like carrot shavings, sweet potato, or fiber-filled goodies.

God loves to see us explore the good gifts (including chocolate) that He's given us. If we enjoy baking, we should try different ways to make new favorites. And we shouldn't be afraid to make mistakes once in a while. The crunchy burned part can always be trimmed away! The point is to have fun. Bake treats no one else has ever made before. Move past the familiar and taste the fantastic.

Lord, show me that it's all right to try new things, to have fun with the good gifts that fill our lives and our stomachs. Let me be willing to open up my mind to creative thinking and enjoy the unexpected results. Amen.

LIES AND MORE LIES

A wicked person listens to deceitful lips;
a liar pays attention to a destructive tongue.
PROVERBS 17:4 NIV

We really can't stop at just one. As hard as we may try, it's not possible to tell a single lie. To bolster the original falsehood, a second is always required. Then a third, fourth, fifth, and the flood becomes unstoppable. Of course, keeping track of all these tales isn't easy either. That's why in the real world, the ploy most often used is to go after the person challenging the lie. No point in coming out and telling the truth, the liar decides. Better to question the questioner and make it seem as though the "innocent" party is above the fray.

How often have we found ourselves in such a sticky situation? We decide that telling a white lie is easier than full disclosure. But somehow it never works out that way, and we end up more entrenched in the sticky web we've woven. Fortunately, the answer is as easy as talking to God about our troubles. By telling the truth, we can stop the cycle of lies quickly.

Famous sports figures, renown politicians, and glamorous movie stars have shown how to "go through the motions" when it comes to whoppers they've told. Some have become quite proficient with their repeated, tearful confessions. But such words mean nothing if they haven't taken things up with God and sought forgiveness.

When we're tempted to take the easy route and cover up instead of come clean, remember that eventually everything will come out. The inevitable disclosure can only be put off for so long. There's no deceiving our Maker, no matter how much and how often we fool ourselves. We need to tell the truth first, and ask questions later. Or we can step into a trap of lying, lying, and lying some more. Sincerity is totally our choice.

Lord, please help me be honest and speak the truth. I want others to trust what I say. Bring into my life examples of great men and women who spoke up for what they believed. Amen.

IGNORING LABELS

Anxiety in a man's heart weighs it down,
but a good word makes it glad.
PROVERBS 12:25 NASB

◄━━━━━

Loser. Fake. Idiot. Fool. These are words we don't like
to hear applied to others, let alone ourselves. And
yet, sometimes we find ourselves smeared with a
mean label that has no connection with who we really
are. Talk about ruining our day! It can be difficult to
overcome the sense of doom and sadness from being
unfairly labeled. And it's hard to scrub that gooey
stuff off our reputations. What a hassle to try to clear
our names.

There's another huge source of these nasty
names. Us. Many times we look back at a bad choice
or an uncomfortable incident with a friend and
think: *He's stupid. What a sicko. He's mean, nasty,*
lame, dim, a phony. The labels come easily, and we
don't even realize that we're bringing pain on both
our target and ourselves. Why do we act this way?
What is it that makes us feel so insecure that we
dare to degrade a beautiful creation of God in such a
negative way? We need to stop tearing people apart

and slandering them with cruel names.

Let's wipe the slate clean. Forget those rude words buzzing around in the background. Ignore the stuff that people have said in the past. Forget the things that have hurt so much but continue to float through our consciousness. Instead, cling tightly to the truths that God has given us. We are forgiven. Joyful. Wonderful. Hopeful. Beautiful. Kind. Compassionate. Caring. These words truly reflect the person within, no matter what others may try to say. Don't let "them" try to plaster us over with unwarranted judgments, shame, and labels. We know who we are and to whom we belong. We are precious in His sight.

God, sometimes I still hurt from a cruel word that cut me to the core. At times I even believe what people say. Help me wipe from my mind what's untrue and replace the negative with positive thoughts from You. Amen.

ACCOUNTING

*"His master replied, 'Well done, good and faithful
servant! You have been faithful with a few things;
I will put you in charge of many things.
Come and share your master's happiness!' "*
MATTHEW 25:21 NIV

When we are called to account for how we spent our
time here on earth, what will we say? It may prove
embarrassing to explain why we chose TV watching
and game playing over building up God's Kingdom.
How will we respond when we think what could have
been accomplished versus how much time we wasted
on silliness? It would be so much better (and easier)
if we just woke up every sunrise with a fresh desire to
serve Him.

Our hope is to one day live forever in heaven.
That's an unchanging and eternal promise that we
can count on. But still, there's that niggling worry that
although our sins are forgiven, perhaps a bit more
is expected of us. We know that our time is limited
on this spinning globe. If we simply spend all our
resources only on ourselves, think only of ourselves,
and do things to promote only ourselves, what good

are we to God? Think of how our perspective would change if we made our top priority to serve God each and every moment. Our humble efforts need not be huge or memorable. What's important is that we are faithfully doing what we've been called to do.

God loves us, but He also wants us to spend our lives wisely. Think how our school years flew by. In a blink, lessons were learned and exams were taken. Then it was on to the next thing. It's a breathless, weary race. And through the fun, the smiles, and the pain, are the questions about how to best live to serve others and the God who made us. If we're faithful to this calling, one day when we stand in heaven, tears gleaming at the glory of His goodness, we shall be commended for doing all that we could.

Oh Lord, will I really be held accountable for every moment of my life? That scares me. Please help me not to waste precious time. And show me how I can do a better job of filling my hours with service to You. Amen.

THE CHOSEN ONE

You did not choose Me, but I chose you and
appointed you that you should go and bear fruit,
and that your fruit should remain, that whatever
you ask the Father in My name He may give you.
JOHN 15:16 NKJV

Every breath is an opportunity to whisper thanks
for being chosen, but we rarely take the time to
reflect on the enormity of the blessing. God set out a
plan that all people should know and love Him and
choose to serve Him. However, He's not going to
force obedience on any of us. That's not the way it
works. We alone make a decision to follow God—or
turn away. All of the details of how we can become
children of the living God can be found in the words
of truth passed down for generations. He loves us!
Yes, the Bible tells us so.

So what does it mean to be chosen? It means that
God persuaded His Son, Jesus, to die for our sins and
the sins of all mankind. That's how much He cares
about us. Of course, that doesn't mean all people
will desire to follow Him. In fact, many will make the
conscious decision to brush Him off, to pull hard in

the other direction when He tugs gently at our hearts.

Each of us is precious in His sight. We can spend eternity in heaven, and no matter what we may have heard otherwise, no sin is too heinous for Him to forgive. But being chosen is only part of the equation. We must accept His gift.

We have been selected for eternal life by the Creator of the universe! It boggles the mind. When we get frustrated by the meaningless details of daily transactions, remember that our whispered prayers are still heard. God wants us to serve Him, and He patiently waits for our response. We can either decide to wholeheartedly accept—or turn down—His gracious proposition. This is the most important decision we will ever make, so let's choose wisely.

God, I'm so small and insignificant, but You care about what I do—or don't do. With all there is to worry about in the world, I'm on Your mind. That makes me stop and think and want to do better for You each moment of every day. Amen.

REMEMBER HIS FAITHFULNESS

Some trust in chariots and some in horses,
but we trust in the name of the LORD our God.
PSALM 20:7 NIV

God's blessings and bounty come in many forms. If we look around, we'll see all the amazing ways God has met our needs. From the sunshine on the leaves to the sweet-smelling rain, He provides. Many times we're given things we hadn't even thought to ask for. How many times have we been anxious about making a loan payment or funding a car repair and any number of other real-world problems, only to see God come through for us? God is in the business of answering prayers both big and little. The answer isn't always "yes," but we can be certain that our best interests are always considered.

Even knowing that, it can still be difficult to trust and believe that all will be well. Perhaps that's because our faith isn't strong enough. When things go well, little faith is required to trust. If the past is any indicator of future difficulties, we may get nervous thinking about what lies ahead. But is worrying necessary or helpful? One way to turn aside from our concerns is to think about the many ways God has provided for us. Even in difficult times, He has provided comfort and sustenance. If we're honest, we can see how we got what we needed exactly when it was needed most.

Journaling provides an excellent opportunity to keep track of the many ways God has been faithful to us. When we're hanging by the thread of prayer, our memories don't always work. That's why it helps to look at a specific written record of what blessings we've enjoyed in the past. Such a reminder boosts our faith. Although it's hard not to worry, trust can be learned. The more we exercise our faith, the more it grows.

Lord, worry comes so easily for me. I want things planned out, figured out, all in a nice, neat row. But that doesn't happen much. Instead, I've got to wait for answers. Please help me to trust Your faithfulness even when I fear, even when I doubt. Amen.

CARING FOR CREATION

The life of every living thing is in His hand,
as well as the breath of all mankind.
JOB 12:10 HCSB

When we care for God's creatures, we are doing exactly what our Maker intended. That's part of the reason family pets can mean so much and provide such pleasure and companionship. Even before we started school, our favorite cat or dog gave us love and concern without asking for a whole lot in return. All that we had to do was provide a safe place to sleep, fresh water, and healthy food. These beloved animals pretty much did the rest.

Not so long ago the idea of caring for God's creation had a whole different meaning. The agricultural lifestyle meant waking up early to feed and milk cattle, muck out horse stalls, shear sheep, and do any number of intense and exhausting chores. Of course, there was always a barn cat and a herding dog in the background, but they weren't around for play so much as to earn their keep. Even today there's a difference of opinion about whether or not animals are meant to serve (and feed) humans or humans are meant to serve and feed them!

In either scenario, we should show responsibility and kindness to the mute creatures committed by God to our care.

Let's reflect on our personal experiences. Are we helping to make this world a safe haven for the animals God put in our lives? It's important that we are. It's also vital to remember that we humans are also unique creations. So when it comes to prioritizing our attention, the special people in our lives deserve lots of love and attention as well. If we find ourselves preferring the company of pets to people, we need to figure out what's wrong and take steps to bring things back into balance again.

Oh God, help me see what spiritual lessons You have for me to learn. Don't let any experience go to waste, but show me that I need to love Your creation and to love You, the Creator. Amen.

BAD STUFF, GOOD PEOPLE

We know that in everything God works for the good of those who love him. They are the people he called, because that was his plan.
ROMANS 8:28 NCV

No doubt at one point or another we've all seen many wonderful people struggle with painful circumstances far beyond their control. Why is the woman who has donated hours to the church stricken with cancer? Why does the young couple begging to be parents hear a resounding "no"? How is it that innocent girls worldwide are stolen from their homes and subjected to slavery? It's because we live in a broken, sin-filled world.

Though it can be difficult, we must trust that in the midst of every bad circumstance some good fruit will be born. We don't understand how that can happen, but in strange and wonderful ways, good arises again and again. Before we start blaming God for causing the problems we complain about, we need to remember that humans have the unique ability to make their own terrible choices. To make decisions that may devastate families for generations. God lets us make up our own minds; without such free will we'd be nothing more than puppets.

We were created to have life and love, not darkness and despair. But difficult things will, and do, happen. Many times we will feel great pain and have confusing questions. We cry out, "Why? This is so unfair!" And it will be, but that doesn't give us a free pass or allow us to say, "Well, this God thing hasn't worked for me, so I'll just indulge in such-and-such sin to relieve my annoyance." We've got to stand up to the one who forces those bad days on us: the destroyer of our souls—not that Satan is to blame for everything bad. We need to accept the truth that sometimes horrible stuff happens to good people—even us—but God is always here to help us through it.

Lord, let me be honest, sometimes it seems like the more I try to serve You, the worse circumstances get for me. That scares me. But I know that You love me and are strengthening my faith. Help me stand firm—no matter what. Amen.

WE'RE NEVER ALONE

What, then, shall we say in response to these things?
If God is for us, who can be against us?
ROMANS 8:31 NIV

———————

There are few things more disappointing than putting ourselves out there and getting nothing back. Like those awkward times when no one responds to our online postings, texts, e-mails, or phone calls. Sure, eventually we might hear something back, but not immediately—and not when we most wanted a supportive response. Perhaps that's because what we call a top priority doesn't necessarily qualify as such to others. Everyone has their tasks and, just like us, an endless to-do list. Is it really reasonable to demand that someone drop everything at our request when we can't do the same for them?

Becoming a servant means putting aside our goals to help someone else. To wipe a child's nose, shovel snow for an elderly neighbor, or wash a pile of dishes. When we think about our neighborhood, city, state, and country, the list of possibilities for service only expands. What's a good-hearted person to do?

First, we must not give up on the great dreams

God has given us to help others. Fighting against tough odds may even be confirmation that we're on the right track. When it comes to demanding action from others, we've got to go easy. We should give a little grace, a little understanding. When someone asks for our help, we should gladly say, "Yes!" Maybe when we pitch in, we'll develop connections that will prove valuable later.

Caring relationships take time. It could be we'll invest a lot for a meager reward. If that's how we see things, we probably need to readjust our attitude. But even if we end up having to tackle the hard stuff by ourselves, let's realize that we still have God on our side. Sometimes that just needs to be enough!

Lord, I can be perfectly happy being served. In fact, I like to forget about what I could and should do and just think about what I want to do. Please help me break through the selfishness to see how I can minister more effectively to others. Amen.

CHOOSE FRIENDS WISELY

In your relationships with one another,
have the same mindset as Christ Jesus.
PHILIPPIANS 2:5 NIV

Once upon a time, life moved more slowly and patience seemed more palatable. These days, though, no one cares to wait. People want what they want when they want it—and that usually means now—or yesterday! Unfortunately, though, it's not possible to have everything immediately unless we're royalty, a celebrity, or both. They're lucky, we think, because they aren't stifled by the need to wait.

In the real world, we sometimes have to delay gratification until something is done cooking, or paid for, or in the budget. That can take awhile, a good long while. But that's okay. What have we done to deserve having all the best stuff instantly anyway? Plus, there's something powerful about savoring a future reward.

The same goes for relationships. We meet someone intriguing and think that we've found the dream partner—or a new best friend. However, once we spend time getting to know that person, we discover we neglected to ask enough questions at the start. And we got stuck with someone with whom we have no meaningful connection. So, of course, the friendship falters because it wasn't carefully considered and has no firm foundation. Rushing ahead with anything, from a purchase to a relationship, often becomes tinged with regret.

Let's promise to take the time we need to get to know who we are. That's the only way we'll understand what's right for us. This doesn't mean we should reject serendipitous connections, but we should be certain that we're not merely trying to add a name to a tally sheet. Instead, we should be working to fill an empty spot in our hearts with the person God intends for us. That takes both time and wisdom, and such valuable commodities cannot be rushed or forced.

Lord, please give me wisdom. Help me to use my gifts and my time wisely. And when it comes to friendships, show me how to share my heart in ways that bring me—and You—great joy. Amen.

TIME TO THINK

*Let it be the hidden person of the heart, with the
imperishable quality of a gentle and quiet spirit,
which is precious in the sight of God.*
1 PETER 3:4 NASB

One of the most undervalued gifts is the opportunity
to be still and silent. In our busy, buzzing world, we
expect background noise. Even our computers, lights,
and fans give off a certain quiet sound that we miss
when they're not powered up. This is the modern age,
so should we really turn everything off and rely on
candlelight? Well, maybe. At least once in a while.

We shouldn't fear peaceful moments alone,
those rare times when we don't have to make
meaningless conversation. There's a certain beauty
to sitting quietly and thinking. It may be difficult
for us to believe, but life *will* go on even without our
invaluable input. Sometimes, in fact, our opinions get
a more serious hearing when we're not always the one
talking. When we take the time to actually listen to
others, what we say comes across as more profound.

There are two good reasons to occasionally
quench the flow of words. First, we need the time to

process our own questions, chart our own course—to wonder, pray, and ask God for help. When we're overwhelmed with noise, we don't have the time to look to the one true Source for assistance. And we can easily get the idea that everything's up to us and that we have to come up with all the answers to save ourselves. But saving ourselves just isn't possible—and it's not going to happen. So we might as well stop pretending.

The second reason? When we use our words sparingly, others are more likely to listen, especially if what we say isn't the first thing that comes into our heads but thoughts carefully considered and worth hearing. Let's begin to value the stillness and find out what we've been missing.

*Oh God, I find it so hard to keep still sometimes.
I feel left out and alone when I'm not caught up
in what everyone else is doing. Teach me to feel
content in prayer, and let me listen carefully
and quietly to Your words for me. Amen.*

CARE FOR THE SICK

*Dear friend, I pray that you may enjoy good
health and that all may go well with you,
even as your soul is getting along well.*
3 JOHN 1:2 NIV

Some of us get queasy around sickness. Even loved
ones can be difficult to care for when they are
struggling with pain, throwing up, or sweaty from
tossing and turning. One reason for our discomfort
is that illness in not the normal state of things. It
was one of the few excuses that kept us home from
school! Sickness confines a person to a cramped
room, while health provides a world of movement
and opportunity. How can we possibly travel, enjoy
friends, or eat what we want when we're experiencing
the annoyance and anguish of disease?

When we're young, illness typically comes
infrequently. We start to feel indestructible. No
matter how many days in a row we've gone without
illness, our lucky streak won't last forever. And when
the inevitable occurs, how will we respond? We need
to accept the fact that sickness happens. It's the way
of a fallen world. Thankfully, most of us don't have

to deal with the down days often or for long, but we need to realize that sometimes, for some people, the pain can last indefinitely.

How we respond to those who are struggling shows us a great deal about our own compassion quotient. If we can't take the time to reach out to those in need, what does that say about our willingness to show care for the hurting? We should not shun those who aren't feeling their best. Instead, we can try to find small, simple ways to encourage those who are down. That might mean sending a card, sharing a favorite song, or giving them a DVD. We can always do something that shows our compassion is consistent even when things aren't going well. That's how they'll know what true friendship (and love) really is.

Dear God, I know that it's tough to feel bad.
Depressing even. But sometimes illness
is the way things are. Help me to count
on You—and share Your love with others,
even when I'm not feeling like it. Amen.

THE SERIOUS SMILE

*Nehemiah said, "Go and enjoy good food and
sweet drinks. Send some to people who have none,
because today is a holy day to the Lord. Don't be sad,
because the joy of the Lord will make you strong."*
NEHEMIAH 8:10 NCV

We all do it sometimes. Put on that "happy face"
though we feel anything but gladness within. That's
completely wrong, right? Well, maybe. There are
times when plastering on a fake smile means we're
trying to fit in or be ignored when we have a less than
optimal attitude. Perhaps this happened during a
tough class in school, for example. But it could also
be that deep down something's hurting us. However,
instead of dealing with the pain, we pretend that
nothing's bothering us. In other words, we lie. This is
definitely not all right.

However, there are other times when bravery
requires a smile even though we can hardly bear to
make our face muscles move. Those are the moments
when we must simply rely on the promises of God to
pull us through. Like when a loved one dies, we lose a
job, or we lose a special relationship.

During such difficulties, there is a deeper strength that allows us to put one foot in front of the other. It is the knowledge that, no matter what, we are loved. That our struggles are seen and our pains are acknowledged. All we can do is rely on what we know of our Creator and continue to trust. That alone allows us to move on.

Sometimes the smile on our face doesn't match reality, and that's all right. In fact, it fits what we know about our source of joy. We know that God remains the same now and forever, and we don't have to rely on mere feelings. Not when we have God's promises. Let's practice the sincere joy of the Lord even when our hearts are aching. The Word of God will give us confidence to know that wherever we go, whatever we do, God is with us.

Dear Lord, at times I feel as though the world is not going the way I want it to. Everything trips me up. When the negatives outweigh the positives, please help me to see that I can trust in You because You are all truth. Amen.

REMEMBER YOUR RAINBOWS

*"Whenever the rainbow appears in the clouds,
I will see it and remember the everlasting
covenant between God and all living
creatures of every kind on the earth."*
GENESIS 9:16 NIV

Every one of us needs to create a personal "rainbow tally sheet." That would be a special list we can review when we fear we've been forgotten. Though at an intellectual level we know that we're constantly loved by the Almighty, there are definitely times when doubts bubble up. Sometimes they grow great enough to snuff out our courage and hope. That's when we need to remember all the great deeds and tiny miracles God has done for us.

Our "rainbow tally" should be detailed and long. The fact that we can breathe, have enough food to fill our stomachs, a warm bed, clothing, transportation, friends, and family should all be included. The list will bolster our weak, often fragmented memories. We should also think of prayers that were answered and jot them down, or times when we gladly grabbed some good news or an immense blessing but forgot to say "thank you."

Let's make it a point every day to think about the proofs, little and large, of God's manifestation in our lives. Even seeing the results of evil in our world can be a strong reminder that the opposite— God's goodness—must truly exist as well. When we have specific answers to prayer, we should rejoice wholeheartedly. Once we start journaling about the amazing answers that have touched our lives through the years, we won't want to stop.

That's because reading over these proofs will do amazing things for our faith. Each line, whether written in sadness or joy, assures us of God's care for us. When we need a boost or reminder, we can pull out our "rainbow tally" and know that the Almighty sees us, loves us, and holds us in His care.

Dear God, Your miracles touch me daily. Things You have done for me and for those I love and for my neighbors, for this land. Please improve my memory, and help me to reflect on Your mercy and the miracles of goodness, and to rejoice in them. Amen.

KEEP CHRISTMAS AND EASTER SPECIAL

Is not the cup of blessing which we bless a sharing in the blood of Christ? Is not the bread which we break a sharing in the body of Christ?
1 CORINTHIANS 10:16 NASB

Without much help we could probably all go off on a rant about how materialism has ruined the celebrations of Christmas and Easter. These Christ-centered holidays have been hijacked by mass merchandisers who use such special days to sell piles of cheap junk and tooth-rotting candies. Santa and the Easter Bunny are the subjects of feature films, while the name of Jesus Christ is pushed into the background, if mentioned at all. What's happening to our culture? What will bring us back to our senses?

As educated adults, we can do our part to celebrate the true significance of the birth and sacrifice of the Savior. It's not enough to attend church twice a year. Rather we should strive to celebrate eternity by reflecting on the birth, death, and resurrection stories all year long. We can see the budding leaves of the maple tree or the short-lived blooms of fragrant cactus flowers and think about new life and the birth of God's one and only Son. Similarly, as winter blankets the brown earth, we can recall how everything must rest, as in death. Spring then comes to remind us of renewal and resurrection.

Let's look for birth and rebirth in the world around us. We can also find it in our own family and relationships. By keeping Christmas and Easter in our hearts, we can do our small part to help others continually remember their meaning and beauty. The breathtaking story of God's love for His creation and of His sacrifice deserves constant retelling. For those of us who already understand their beauty, we can continually rejoice in the good glorious news. For those of us who don't understand these intricacies, the Bible holds the key to grasping the greatness of the most amazing gift imaginable.

Jesus, the beauty of celebrating Your life, death, and resurrection can be a constant in my life. Help me not to just think of You at Christmas and Easter, but instead let me understand Your majesty all year round. Amen.

THE CENTER OF THE UNIVERSE

You show that you are a letter from Christ,
the result of our ministry, written not with ink
but with the Spirit of the living God, not on tablets
of stone but on tablets of human hearts.
2 CORINTHIANS 3:3 NIV

Watching TV or reading a current biography, one
might think that humans are the center of the
universe and that they can control and do anything.
Of course, that isn't the case, but what is for certain is
that modern man is convinced of his greatness and
supposed ability to do anything under the sun.

Despite our willingness to believe the best
about ourselves, most of us know deep down that
we are really nothing more than tiny specks in the
vastness of the stretching universe. However, we have
another foundation for our value and worth that is far
more meaningful and lasting. That's our position as
children of God. It's true that we are tiny in the realm
of nature and the cosmos, but so what? We can hold
on to God's promises and live a life full of meaning
and purpose, or we can foolishly try to carve out our
own niche of significance. That's like creating a

mini-mountain of ice cream. It might be impressive on the dining room table, but once it begins to melt, our efforts become mere mush.

Let's allow God to guide us to a place of value and meaning. He loves us and will lead us on paths of righteousness if only we're willing to forgo the fantasy that we are the most important presence on the planet and accept that we are the searching children of a loving God and can only find fulfillment and full joy when we choose to follow His will.

Thanks, dear Lord, for seeing me and loving me though I am small in the grand scheme of things. Please give me eternal significance by my connection to You. Thanks for reaching down and pulling me up to a place of love and peace. Amen.

TEARS ARE OKAY

You have recorded my troubles.
You have kept a list of my tears.
Aren't they in your records?
PSALM 56:8 NCV

Some of us were taught that it's not okay to cry under any circumstance. Male or female, we're supposed to be tough and stoic though our world is falling apart. Allowing a teardrop to fall would be inappropriate because it means we've lost control. No one wants that. In a world where weakness is frowned upon, who wants to appear vulnerable?

Of course, there's another way of looking at the situation. In reality, often the individuals who are unable to let go emotionally are also poor at connecting. Those who are never touched by another person's story find that they can't bond with anyone else because they refuse to open their hearts. They shut out their gift of empathy.

There once was a man who decided that he would never allow a single person to touch his soul. He'd been hurt as a child and vowed never to let that happen again. So he worked hard to keep all human emotion at arm's length. He'd keep a stiff upper lip and maintain a safe distance. No hugs, no hand-holding. And no one would ever have the slightest peek at his heart. For years he lived this way, emotionally apart, always watching from the outside. He never joined in.

When he grew old and reached his last days, he wondered why there was no one near. Where was the consolation he sought? Perhaps he was lonely because he never allowed anyone to see inside. He never bonded in any meaningful, loving way. His was a sad conclusion to a long, solitary life. Without sharing our hearts, our loves, and a tear or two at times, we miss the chance to be whole and wholly human.

Lord, I want my heart to sense the needs of others. Please allow me to show empathy to others, to feel their pain, and to care about those in my life in the way I want them to care about me. Amen.

WHAT'S INSIDE?

"Whoever believes in me, as Scripture has said, rivers of living water will flow from within them."
JOHN 7:38 NIV

Why is it so simple to sneer? Probably because we've had various people model such behavior throughout our lives. On many media programs, we've seen people striking poses, copping attitudes, and living large. They teach viewers that one of the best ways to stand at the top is to bring someone else down. Perhaps that's why cutting remarks are so popular in school and on the streets. Such words *do* make others feel small and unimportant, but looking down on the less fortunate only increases the supposed importance of those playing the same insult game, not the rest of us.

Convincing others that they're less than awesome (and certainly less valuable, pretty, handsome, caring, smart, wealthy, fill-in-the-blank than we are) doesn't raise us up. Instead, it strips them of their pride and dignity. We do that when we look down on those whom God has created. Because His imprint is on their souls, they are special and beautiful, even if we refuse to see it. We completely overlook what's really important when we become obsessed with outward appearances.

What's inside a person matters. Immense creativity can flow from a person who is severely handicapped. An angel's voice can emanate from a person whose appearance is plain and unpolished. It's the relationship we share with God, the mighty Maker of the universe that makes us amazing. When we are willing to see that inner glory in others, all mankind is lifted up.

We can try to fool ourselves into thinking that our own fleeting looks, abilities, or wealth make us worthwhile, but what happens when those things disappear or are stripped away by accident or aging? Only what's within remains. But if we nurture that inner strength and beauty, we are left with a life that is truly worth living.

Dear Lord, please help me see beyond the surface. When I look in the mirror help me focus on the person You want me to be inside. Help me to see the beauty in others that comes from deep within.

BODY BASICS

*"The eye is the lamp of the body.
If your eyes are healthy,
your whole body will be full of light."*
MATTHEW 6:22 NIV

Despite what we may have thought during those not-so-long-ago study sessions, the body cannot possibly go nonstop without ultimately paying a high price, and energy drinks aren't the answer. We may temporarily feel invincible and superpowered, but time catches up eventually.

Now is when we should establish patterns of good rest, eating nutritious food, and limiting stress in our lives. Sleep is our friend, so we've got to be sure we're getting enough. And as the years pass and metabolism slows, we need to eat food that is good for us, food that keeps us moving without bulking us up. Finally, though some stress can be good, even motivating, too much stress will negate other gains we've achieved.

We should take honest stock of how we're living our lives. Caring for ourselves, body and soul, is a sacred responsibility and not always an easy one.

There are often more talkers than doers when it comes to keeping up with healthy pursuits. The best approach would be to find some activity, whether it's walking, biking, swimming, hiking, or some other outside endeavor, and partake in it regularly. This will definitely decrease stress and increase the enjoyment of life. Finding a friend to enjoy the outdoors with us also increases motivation.

Here are a few other simple hints that can help us to live healthy lives: Exercise, drink plenty of water, and eat good-for-you foods and only when hungry, stopping when full. It goes without saying, we should avoid smoking, illicit drugs, and excess alcohol. Finally, we should nurture our souls along with our bodies. That's the best way to keep things in balance and ourselves full of all goodness.

Lord, please help me take care of this amazing body You've given me. What an incredible gift! Help me to be healthy and to find ways to care for myself so that I can serve You better. Amen.

CLING TO THE TRUTH

"What is truth?" retorted Pilate. With this he went out again to the Jews gathered there and said, "I find no basis for a charge against him."
JOHN 18:38 NIV

What is truth? The question has been asked in every generation with varying degrees of sincerity. Another good query is this: Where is truth hiding? For example, it's difficult to find honest news because almost every resource is either sponsored by an advertiser or written to promote someone's popularity or peculiar worldview. Sometimes, to get at the truth, it helps to skip the mainstream perspective, go directly to the source, and make our own decisions.

For believers, that means reading the Bible and trusting that those precious words matter. Trust that they amount to something real and important and worth following. Many people think they can pick and choose truth when it comes to God's Word. What works for them personally is accepted without question, but if the truth pricks their conscience, they skip it and move on to something less challenging.

That is how proof-texting works. A person decides he or she wants to hold a certain belief and then goes through the Bible finding only the verses that support that specific point of view. Anything that conflicts with that unique perspective is ignored. Of course, proof-texting ignores truth with a capital "T." It merely bolsters one's personal opinion with manipulated quotations.

We can trust God's Word and its inherent honesty. In a world where it's considered shocking to challenge someone's personal perspective, we must be willing to acknowledge that some things are true and some things aren't. Period. Logically, that means two people with opposing opinions can't both be right. And neither can a whole array of viewpoints all be correct. There is a right and a wrong, a true and a false. For believers, we need to find the truth in God's Word, stick to it, and never look back.

Lord, please let me be a voice for the truth.
Help me not to be afraid to stand up for what
I believe and to trust that Your Word is all
I need to know that truth. Amen.

PRAY FIRST

I have called upon You, for You will hear me, O God;
incline Your ear to me, and hear my speech.
PSALM 17:6 NKJV

Where does prayer fit into our moment-by-moment plans? The memories of school and graduation day are still fresh. Throughout our educational experience, we certainly faced days we wished we could have skipped. Challenges loomed in the form of exams, papers, expenses, and projects. And there will be many more ahead.

What was our first reaction when we got a tough, new assignment? Hopefully, it was to whisper a quick prayer for clarity and creativity. Even though we know better, asking God for help isn't always our first response. We sometimes might even dare to think He's a little too busy to be worried about our little problems. That thought couldn't be further from the truth.

When it comes to life, the bigger the task, the greater will be our success when we triumph—or the louder the crash should we fail. If and when the latter occurs, we can't give up. But we can learn.

On a practical level, we can seek out a helping hand, encouragement, or advice from a friend. On a spiritual level, what should always come first is prayer. We should ask for clear thinking and wisdom as we move ahead.

God stands ready to help us, no matter what our circumstances. But we shouldn't wait until things start falling apart. God will provide strength, wisdom, and support even when things are going well. All we have to do is request His help.

When it comes to decision making, let's commit to pray first. That's always a good plan, no matter what we've got to tackle. And often we're as delighted as we are surprised at what we can accomplish when we check in with God rather than roaring blindly ahead on our own.

Lord, please show me how I can accomplish good and great things for You. Everything always works best when I involve You early on. Give me wisdom and direction, and show me how to ask for and find the help I need. Amen.

ACTS OF KINDNESS

I led them with cords of human kindness, with ties of love. To them I was like one who lifts a little child to the cheek, and I bent down to feed them.
HOSEA 11:4 NIV

The best advice for improving the kindness quotient in our lives is to take note when we're on the receiving end of such goodness. How does it make us feel when someone gives us a quick wave when we open up a space for them in traffic? Or when our neighbor asks how we're doing? Seeing a handwritten letter of encouragement from a parent or loved one can also make our day.

Being kind to those we consider our enemies (or the people who make our lives much more miserable than necessary) is not easy. We'd rather talk about those people behind their backs and dig up dirt on their lives. This could apply to the boss who continually hands out weekend assignments or the coworker determined to steal our glory. Is it even possible to show kindness to such undeserving folks?

Perhaps the best approach is to climb off whatever pedestal we've scrambled onto. We've got a lot of nerve looking down at others. Remember, if we got exactly what we deserved, well, that wouldn't be a pretty picture. Humbling ourselves to offer small kindnesses to those who drive us crazy is a type of do-it-yourself heart surgery. It's quite a character-building operation.

Simple ways to share kindness include greeting people by name and showing them the respect they deserve (even if we don't think they are worthy of it). Most of all, it's important to be sincere. We waste our time, effort, and breath when we try to coerce people into thinking we care about them. It's crazy to think they can't tell the difference. Instead, we must show the kindness and compassion that comes from God. That's what changes our hollow gestures into something so powerful it can change a life.

Lord, I have a hard time sometimes with the difficult people in my life. Please give me the grace and energy to try to be kind to those who aren't very kind to me. Amen.

MUST SIN PREVAIL?

Therefore, submit to God.
But resist the Devil, and he will flee from you.
JAMES 4:7 HCSB

Lots of us think that we're pretty tough when it comes to resisting temptation. We don't ever *have* to give in, we tell ourselves. Just gut it out and we can get through anything. Over the years, our glorious victories shine, but the moments we've faltered still sting. Perhaps pride tripped us up and made us overlook our weaknesses. Maybe we didn't ask God for help because we thought we had it all under control.

The secret to avoiding sin isn't difficult. We make it more complicated by playing little games like seeing how close we can come to the edge without toppling over. Whose fault is that? Not God's. To stand up against Satan's wiles, we need to determine in advance the path we'll pursue. Do we want to spend our earthly existence worrying about whether or not we'll go to heaven, or do we want to live each day in service to God? The choice is clear, but still we waver. We've known since we started school that we shouldn't watch a certain type of movie or hang out with a specific type of "friend," but we do it anyway because it makes us feel like part of the cool crowd.

Avoiding temptations is about doing what's right even when we don't feel like it, even when we are tired, afraid, and angry. In order to have the strength to push against the hard things that crop up, we must have a solid foundation in the truth and realize that our faith allows us to ask God for help anytime, any place. That's the secret. Being ready for the inevitable and praying for backup even before we think we need it.

*Lord, I want to follow You, but sometimes
I find myself running in the wrong direction.
Please draw me nearer and give me what I need
to stay on Your straight and narrow path. Amen.*

LOVE POTION

"Do not seek revenge or bear a grudge against anyone among your people, but love your neighbor as yourself. I am the LORD."
LEVITICUS 19:18 NIV

Believe it or not, having the "greats"—great hair, great car, great clothes, and great skin—won't necessarily bring that perfect someone into our lives. There is no magic potion. True, we all want to feel wanted and needed. However, too many of us are willing to cross any line, take any chance, to draw a potential mate nearer. When we treat relationships as a game, there are bound to be both winners and losers.

Only God's love is guaranteed. All of the other earthly arrangements result from two flawed individuals trying to create a loving bond. It's no surprise that such connections are fraught with confusion and complexity. It's also no wonder we're so wary. We can all point to excellent bad examples of relationships, like we saw in school perhaps. Most of us also have a tear-stained list of family members, friends, neighbors, and coworkers whose relationships are examples of how things can go very wrong.

The pursuit of love is not for the weak. Many of us have seen our hopes and dreams squashed because we miscalculated and bet on a fickle heart. Yet, thankfully, people still try. Sometimes they even find exactly what both partners want and need.

As with all good things, our model for love should arise from what we know of God's love for us. His example is amazing. It reflects self-sacrifice and a pure focus on what is best for us. Not only does God provide for our basic needs of shelter, warmth, air, food, and water, but He cares about our goals and the heartfelt desire for fulfillment and joy. No matter what hurts we harbor or what pain we push down, God loves us. When we accept that truth, we'll see amazing things happen in all of our relationships.

Lord, I feel hopeless sometimes. I wonder if I'm meant to find happiness and love. Please let me see that You will always be there for me. Thank You for loving me no matter what. Amen.

TRULY SORRY

"Forgive us our debts,
as we also have forgiven our debtors."
MATTHEW 6:12 NASB

Hurting someone's feelings isn't difficult. It can be done efficiently with just a few sharp, cutting words. Throughout our school experience, we've heard others shred teachers, professors, and public figures with vicious words. Sometimes we might have had the courage to speak up to defend a cause or person we cared about—or we may have listened, wondering what it would take to make someone regret their unkindness.

As important as apologies are, nasty negative words, once spoken, can never be completely erased. Though the "I'm sorry" may numb the pain, the mean speech still burns like barbs of venom. Just spouting that magic phrase of regret may not be enough to restore a relationship.

No. It takes more than asking for forgiveness. It takes moving ahead with deliberate, dedicated plans to restore the broken ties. The person at the other end of our unkind words may have a hard time believing that we're really sorry, especially if we continue to treat him or her with disrespect.

A wise option is to always avoid saying anything we'll come to regret. To never spout off anything we wouldn't want overheard or shared online. However, that's probably less than realistic. So when our self-control slips, we need to confess what we've done and ask for forgiveness. Never, under any circumstances, should we use waffle words like "I'm sorry if you feel I've offended you." That's insincere and pointless, and it weakly attempts to shift our guilt to the person to whom we've been cruel.

When an "I'm sorry" is required, we should say it. And we should explain what we're sorry for and why. Then, over time, we can show we really mean it by never repeating the circumstances that forced the apology in the first place.

Dear Lord, it's really hard for me to apologize to certain people. Sometimes I wrongly feel they do deserve to hear what I said, no matter how unkind. But help me to know when I've been cruel and to avoid hurting people with words. Amen.

MUSIC MATTERS

As they make music they will sing,
"All my fountains are in you."
PSALM 87:7 NIV

God gave us some things for pure pleasure. Music, for example, can be enjoyed by the young, the old, the professional, and the self-taught. When we listen to the sounds of birds singing, brooks babbling, waves crashing, and raindrops clattering, we get a sense of the emotional variety evoked by these remarkable rhythms and melodies. Today's musical options are enormous. Songs have been created from other musical styles. Music once sung in taverns gets new lyrics and is recycled for churches. We never know how the soul of man may pick up and reuse the music of others. That's what makes it so amazingly creative.

The types of instruments that have been made to create joyful noise and jangling metallic sounds seem endless in their variety as well. Some music soothes us, some excites, and some saddens. From a rousing military stanza to a wedding march, music touches every aspect of our lives. People enjoy music while commuting, studying, exercising, cooking, cleaning, gardening, and reading. We all have a sound track that speaks to us specifically, and we love to have it playing on an iPod or whatever musical source best delivers the sounds we crave. Music also moves us. Certain songs have helped us get through hard times, especially those treasured riffs that mean more to us than words can convey.

Enjoy music as a sound-drenched present from the Creator. With so many opportunities and outlets for this amazing gift, we are able to find something that suits us. Share music with friends and family, realizing that we are all touched in different ways by different melodies. Every once in a while, let's turn everything off and open our ears to the music of nature, the music that God created and the sounds that inspire the soul.

*Lord, help me to hear You in the variety of music
I enjoy. I love so many kinds! Thanks for giving me
the chance to enjoy my life even more because
I can hear Your beauty in music. Amen.*

MIGHTY MOUSE

I am afraid that, as the serpent deceived Eve by his craftiness, your minds will be led astray from the simplicity and purity of devotion to Christ.
2 CORINTHIANS 11:3 NASB

So who's afraid of a tiny little mouse? That huge elephant, for one. For years we have heard how towering pachyderms can be thrown into a frenzy by a close encounter with the tiny rodent. It's amusing to picture such enormous animals running around wildly because of a puny mouse. Maybe mice, especially the electronic kind, have more power than we think.

Once we make the decision to work on a computer, we can create all sorts of amazing things: sparkling résumés, love poems, short stories, novels, screenplays, and how-to manuals. It's up to us what we type and what spills out onto the paper. However, when we decide to turn onto the information highway, that Mighty Mouse can lead us into all sorts of sordid spots. Trashy locations we have no business exploring open their doors wide with but a quick click of the mouse.

The scary thing is, after we wallow in the garbage for a while, we may stop noticing the smell. Mighty Mouse seems to take over our good sense, and we find ourselves roaming where we have no business going. We need to learn to control that tool, or else!

Of course, we can't blame a little mouse for leading us away from the straight and narrow path. Nope. That's all on us. We choose when we want to click on something, what we want to click on, and what direction we want to go. Why not use our computer and the massive resources available online to expand our knowledge base and draw us closer to God? Or we can choose to let our minds wander and temptations take over as we scramble astray. Greater purity or putridity are the only outcomes. It's up to us.

Lord, please keep my mind and heart pure from all the distractions so readily available in the computer world. Forgive me when I stray, and help me keep within the boundaries that are good and right for me. Amen.

TREASURE TROVE

Store up for yourselves treasures in heaven,
where moths and vermin do not destroy,
and where thieves do not break in and steal.
MATTHEW 6:20 NIV

One dark night we hear a huge crash in the backyard. Yep, it's space aliens, and they've landed their super-sleek cruiser on the grass. The pair comes to the glass patio door and knocks. Green-skinned, thin, and grinning, they each carry a clipboard. They're not asking to see our leader but simply want to survey our stuff. In the interest of intergalactic communications, we agree to let them tour our place—we're proud of how well everything's kept up. The two step inside, long feet flopping on the tile.

First, they look through the kitchen pantry at the amazing store of foods from every land. Every spice imaginable stands ready. Plus the juicer, pasta maker, microwave, stove, oven, fridge with ice maker, disposal, trash compactor, bread machine, and multi-speed vents. Lots of time-saving devices, we muse, but not so much extra time.

Next, the tall green guys stop in the living room

and jot down notes about our electronic equipment, the surround-sound speakers, the Blu-ray player, the wall-sized flat-screen facing heavy recliners with indents for soda cans and brimming snack trays. "Impressive," we hear. They go from room to room, filling their notepads. They leave shaking their heads as they say, "Farewell, Earthlings," and head off for their next galaxy.

As we wave, thoughts spin through our minds. What is that weird feeling in the pit of our stomachs? We sense that the aliens didn't quite approve of our lifestyle. There's nothing wrong with having cool stuff, right? We could give away everything if someone asked. Maybe we could live more simply and enjoy what we have without worrying about our next purchase? It's an alien thought all right. Maybe it's time to start doing our own room-to-room survey.

Lord, please help me to understand when enough is enough. When I look around my room, my house, my car, I see so much. More than I need. I am sorry when I keep trying to get more stuff rather than living contently here and now. Amen.

HEADING TO HEAVEN?

He will destroy death forever.
The Lord GOD will wipe away the tears from
every face and remove His people's disgrace
from the whole earth, for the LORD has spoken.
ISAIAH 25:8 HCSB

No one wants to talk about death. It's hardly worth thinking about it while we're young. We just graduated, right? Many incredible possibilities await us. In fact, here's exactly how it will work: One stage of life will prepare us for the next. We will move up the ladder at work, find the love of our lives, take awesome vacations, get a dog or cat, raise a family, and see firsthand what it means to be upwardly mobile! We want the good stuff, the happy stuff. Everything that's usual and expected.

At least it would be, if not for the fact that things often change. We can't know from one day to the next what might turn out differently than we expected.

Not everyone finds a spouse, some people never land their fantasy job, and not everyone has all their dreams come true. We do know this: every "Once upon a time" story closes with "The End." That's for certain. Are we living with God's will hardwired into our spiritual GPS? If not, now is the time to make a course adjustment. We shouldn't wait until we're heading toward shore on that final, slow wave.

Life is a breathtaking mix of exciting transitions, wonderful blessings, and scary moments. But no matter what pattern our individual ups and downs take, a time will come when we all stand before the Creator to answer the question, "Why do you belong in heaven?" And by that point, the choice between living in His presence eternally or living a life of dark separation from Him will already have been made. The decisions leading to that critical final exam are formulated each and every moment of each and every day.

Lord, I look forward to heaven! Please show me how I can live my life now in such a way that draws me nearer to You. Help me to see Your amazing goodness and gifts and to plainly see Your plan for me. Amen.

Scripture Index

OLD TESTAMENT

NEW TESTAMENT